T0064445

STRATEGIC CORPORATE SUSTAINABILTY™

Strategic Corporate Sustainability
7 Imperatives for Sustainable Business

R.A. FERNANDO

Editor: Dana Dyer Pierson

PARTRIDGE

Strategic Corporate Sustainability

" A Commitment to implementing strategies for Sustainable Business which differentiates the organization, whilst impacting all stakeholders which are in its sphere of influence" © Ravi Fernando January 2010

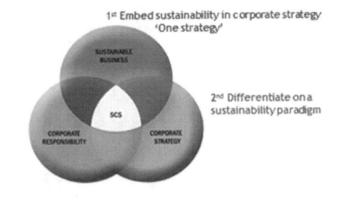

1st Embed sustainability in corporate strategy 'One strategy'

2nd Differentiate on a sustainability paradigm

US Copyright © Ravi Fernando TX 7 -180-253 of January 31, 2010

Copyright © 2015 by R.A. Fernando.

ISBN: Hardcover   978-1-4828-5404-6
           Softcover   978-1-4828-5403-9
           eBook   978-1-4828-5405-3

All rights reserved. No part of this book may be used or reproduced by any means, graphic, electronic, or mechanical, including photocopying, recording, taping or by any information storage retrieval system without the written permission of the author except in the case of brief quotations embodied in critical articles and reviews.

Because of the dynamic nature of the Internet, any web addresses or links contained in this book may have changed since publication and may no longer be valid. The views expressed in this work are solely those of the author and do not necessarily reflect the views of the publisher, and the publisher hereby disclaims any responsibility for them.

Print information available on the last page.

To order additional copies of this book, contact
Toll Free 800 101 2657 (Singapore)
Toll Free 1 800 81 7340 (Malaysia)
orders.singapore@partridgepublishing.com

www.partridgepublishing.com/singapore

If a business is to pursue *strategic corporate sustainability*,[1] its leadership needs to make a commitment to mainstream sustainability as the central focus of its corporate strategy. Thereafter, create one strategy that will guide and direct the business.

The business needs to follow a two-step process:

1) **Embed sustainability** in every element of the strategy, and *'sustainability-proof'* it.

The strategy must be augmented with an *environmental strategy* that helps the business achieve carbon neutrality.

2) **Differentiate** the product, service, or offering on a *sustainability paradigm* and invest in strategic innovation to create sustainable value.

A commitment to strategic corporate sustainability is a strategic decision that moves away from 'bolt-on' CSR and sustainability initiatives.

---

[1] FERNANDO. R (2012), Sustainable globalization, Journal of Corporate Governance Vol.12 No.4 2012 pp.586

To my late father, **Lancelot Aelian Fernando,** in appreciation of his intellectual foresight and inspiration

CONTENTS

The Reality
Global Sustainability Challenges

The Reality
Corporate Response
to Sustainability Challenges

The Challenge
Strategic Corporate Sustainability

The Opportunity
Strategic Corporate Sustainability
Seven Imperatives for Sustainable Business

The Future
A Call to Action
for a Sustainable Planet!

ABOUT THE AUTHOR

 R.A. Fernando is an alumnus of the University of Cambridge (Wolfson College), having completed his post-graduate certificate in sustainable business in 2008–09 and master of studies in sustainable leadership in 2014. He also holds an MBA from the University of Colombo and is a fellow of the Chartered Institute of Marketing (UK). At the INSEAD Business School (France), he completed a diploma in international management and the Advanced Management Programme. He is a doctor of business administration candidate at the European Business School in Geneva.

He is the operations director of the Malaysia Blue Ocean Strategy Institute. His career with multinationals including Unilever, Sterling Health International, and Smithkline Beecham International covered Africa, the Middle East, and Asia in CEO and marketing positions between 1981 and 2003. He was the first CEO of SLINTEC (Sri Lanka Institute of Nanotechnology) from 2008 to 2010.

He was also the United Nations global compact focal point for Sri Lanka 2003–2010 and founder of UN Global Compact Sri Lanka in 2010.

In academia, he was a visiting faculty member of the INSEAD Advanced Management Programme between 2005 and 2010 and on the current faculty of CEDEP (European Centre for Executive Development). He has been an executive in residence at the INSEAD Social Innovation Centre from September 2010 to the present day. He is also a visiting faculty member at the Deusto Business School, Universtat of Pompeu Fabra in Spain, and University of Colombo MBA programs, where he teaches Strategic Corporate Sustainability. Babson College USA published three Giving Voice to Values cases on his work in Kenya and Vietnam.

In September 2007, he won a Global Strategy Leadership award at the World Strategy Summit for his work on sustainability-led branding.

At the Global Strategy summit with Professor Renée Mauborgne (INSEAD)   At Cambridge University

FOREWORD

Over the past century, unprecedented economic growth has led to ever-rising prosperity for the middle and upper classes across the globe, and lifted many (but far from all) of the world's poorest out of extreme poverty. However, it has also resulted in a number of interrelated economic, social, and environmental challenges that have serious consequences for how societies will develop for the foreseeable and distant future. The impact of the global financial crisis will be felt for decades; climate change is already affecting the livelihoods of many around the globe, ecosystems are rapidly declining, and a rapidly growing population is putting strain on existing patterns of resource use and food production.[2]

This poses critical questions for all actors and institutions in society about their role in shaping a more sustainable and equitable society on a finite planet. For business, these questions are particularly prominent, as it is directly connected to the resource use and labour conditions for the production of the goods and services that drive the current unsustainable consumption patterns.

However, for many businesses, this is not necessarily obvious; their executives don't see how they are implicated or consider their role in the value chain too limited to drive action. Even for those who do understand the predicament, the question is how to translate this into practical action within their organisations and

---

[2] World Economic Forum (2015) Global Risks Report; KPMG (2013) Expect the Unexpected.

how to relate to the broad set of stakeholders that are touched by the company's activities.[3]

In this context, terms like 'corporate (social) responsibility' and 'sustainability' have become ubiquitous concepts to denote attempts to manage a host of core and peripheral issues that arise from doing business. Yet for many business leaders, it remains a challenge to balance the interests of different stakeholders in practice, let alone how to develop a sustainable strategy and organisation. It is unfamiliar terrain, and yet it is of strategic importance to secure long-term access to strategic resources, the ability to respond adequately to looming socioeconomic shifts, social and regulatory license to operate, and the enduring profitability of the business, to name but a few.

The executives who do want to embark on the journey towards a more sustainable firm and society are therefore faced with a big challenge, as merely adding a green label on a product or launching a philanthropic campaign clearly won't be sufficient to do this seriously and for the long run. Rather, to leave a lasting legacy, it is essential to embed sustainability into the structure and activities of the firm – into its DNA.

To support this transformation, R.A.Fernando has written an excellent book based on his experience at the UN Global Compact and corporations like Unilever, Sterling Health, and Smithkline Beecham, and his studies at the University of Cambridge Institute for Sustainability Leadership. The argument is simple: to ensure

---

[3]   UNGC/Accenture (2013) The UN Global Compact-Accenture CEO Study on Sustainability 2013

the long-term commitment of a company, it is essential that sustainability is integrated in a number of ways; and for each of these aspects, there are some clear considerations that need to be resolved. The resulting process of change in the organisation will build a more resilient business that can not only cope with the challenges ahead but can start capturing different forms of value from a sound sustainability strategy by protecting the value of the business through risk management; improving the returns on capital through operational efficiencies and sustainable value chains; and growing the business through innovation, new business models, and new markets.[4]

Strategic Corporate Sustainability - 7 Imperatives for Sustainable Business is not a 'how to' book; it doesn't prescribe a golden set of rules. Any attempt at this would be quite futile, given that every company context is unique. Rather, it provides a clear map of what needs to be addressed, and as such, the book serves as a guide for the journey towards a company that has sustainability thinking at its heart. In this respect, it is particularly valuable that R.A.Fernando has included thoughts on what will be and what won't be helpful in the implementation of the imperatives, as these can be useful starting points for engagement with the appropriate managers, employees, and external stakeholders to start defining how the company will put them into practice.

The journey towards a more sustainable company and society is not an easy task - it will be a demanding process that requires genuine leadership, a clear vision and perseverance, and a

---

[4] Bonini .S & Görner .S (2014) The Business of Sustainability: Putting it into Practice. McKinsey & Co.

homegrown implementation for which there is no manual. This book will be an essential guide to writing your own.

Dr Maarten van der Kamp
Managing Director, Value in Enterprise Limited
Cambridge, 15 July 2015

The willingness to practice strategic corporate sustainability as a strategy approach for organisations must start with an urgent awareness of the need and importance of changing their current business model to a sustainable business model as the only way of doing business, in order to ensure that their pursuit of economic benefit does not imperil society and the environment locally and globally in the very near future.

This requires the determination and development of a sustainability mindset in business leaders, and it is also their responsibility to encourage and develop their respective stakeholders, in order to establish a sustainability culture that will benefit their organisation, the welfare of society, and the environment in the future.

R.A.Fernando is extremely passionate about delivering his core message on the importance of establishing sustainable business model, and his book, *Strategic Corporate Sustainability – 7 Imperatives for Sustainable business,* serves as an excellent guide to inspire business leaders to develop a sustainability mindset and focus on the seven key imperatives required for developing their respective sustainable business models.

I am certain that this book would be the catalyst that can create a considerable impact on business practices globally but perhaps more so in Asia, which is experiencing rapid growth and industrialisation.

Peter Ooi, Phd
Global Leadership Academy, Malaysia
24 July 2015

PREFACE

The rising influence of business directly impacts global sustainability, as business is a key driver of resource utilisation and an influencer of national policy. This makes it imperative for business leaders to be sensitive to global sustainability challenges. The perception amongst non-business leaders and academics is that most business leaders continue with business as usual, as articulated below.

- 'How concerned are CEOs about climate change?[5] Not at all, our economic system enriches the powerful at the expense of the 99 per cent. It is profitable to let the world go to hell,' says Jorgen Randers, professor of climate strategy at Norwegian Business School.
- 'Oil companies are insisting on their right to use our atmosphere as an open sewer,' says Al Gore

Have leaders in academia, business schools, and global agencies been able to bring about a tipping point amongst business or national leaders to integrate sustainability in strategy? Have they been educated, inspired, and motivated to create sustainable business? Have they been schooled in taking decisions through the prism of the triple bottom line with a sense of urgency to avert climate change? Have we *challenged* business to create new sustainable products and services in a world of unsustainable portfolios? Have we inspired business with the *opportunity* to

---

[5] Guardian 20th January 2015: How concerned are CEO's about Climate change?

create new blue oceans of uncontested green market spaces that will grow rapidly? Have we engaged and inspired them to impact the global sustainability challenges, i.e., millennium development goals (1990-2014), or new UN sustainable development goals as a key component of their strategy? Have we put in place a global reward system that gives business an opportunity to change from the quarterly performance syndrome to strategic performance? The answer is a resounding *no!* Yes, we have a few exceptions to the rule – Unilever, Interface, Tesla, and General Electric – but the majority is yet to start the journey. Then it dawned on me that most business schools are yet to include sustainability as a subject in the MBA curriculum. Can we blame business for driving shareholder value or pursuing short-term economic growth utilising all available resources as taught in business schools? Is it realistic for us to expect today's business leaders and boards to be sensitive to a subject that was not in the curriculum when they were in business school twenty to thirty years ago?

It was in 1987 that the term 'sustainable development' gained prominence with the Bruntland Report, and in 1997, John Elkington coined the term 'triple bottom line'. I reflected on what was needed to change the status quo.

Embedding sustainability in an organisation's corporate strategy could be the game changer.[6] However, it was reported by Corporate Knights Capital (2014-15) that only 3 per cent of the world's largest

---

[6]   Ethical Corporation (January 2015) Top Sustainability trends for 2015

4,609 listed business entities even report sustainability, whilst 97 per cent don't;[7] this is a key indicator of the reality.

Today, the majority of business leaders assume corporate responsibility should be confined to corporate social responsibility (CSR) and that macro sustainability issues are the domain of governments. However, the new paradigm for corporate responsibility is a business's commitment to sustainable business.[8] Doing good and doing well as opposed doing good to look good has to be the new approach. Minimising the ecological, carbon, and water footprint business has on the planet has to be a key focus. Today, global sustainability issues pose an unprecedented threat to the survival of business as usual. If business does not address the risks posed by emerging sustainability challenges, neither the business nor the planet will survive. CSR is only the stepping stone for embracing triple-bottom-line sustainability.

Strategic corporate sustainability is the recommended approach for embedding sustainability in corporate strategy. It is achieved when business first recognises the urgent need to embed and internalise sustainability in corporate strategy as its central guiding principle. This key step will lead to a second step, where the 'sustainable innovation and differentiation' of its products and services strive to create sustainable value. This twin commitment will ensure that business impacts its sphere of influence sustainably from a strategic perspective. The Seven

---

[7] Confino .J (2014) 19 October 2014 - Finance hub from Guardian Sustainable Business

[8] FERNANDO. R (2012), Sustainable globalization, Journal of Corporate Governance Vol.12 No.4 2012

Imperatives are the steps enlightened businesses mobilised in their journey towards strategic corporate sustainability.

To achieve the goal, we needed to have first educated business leaders how sustainable business creates sustainable value. Encourage them to pursue sustainability as a business growth opportunity, to create new 'green market spaces' in a fossil-fuel-based global economy full of unsustainable products and services. I focused on identifying key imperatives from best practices on how it has been done. My focus at Cambridge University's Institute of Sustainability Leadership (2007-2014) attached to Wolfson College was to find answers to help business leaders 'embed sustainability in corporate strategy'. *Strategic Corporate Sustainability – 7 Imperatives for Sustainable Business* is the result of this journey.

ACKNOWLEDGMENTS

My journey to write *Strategic Corporate Sustainability - 7 Imperatives for Sustainable Business* has had many direct and indirect influencers, each of whom has played a key role, and I want to acknowledge their contribution.

I want to start by expressing my sincere gratitude to Dr Maarten Van der Kamp, whom I first met at Cambridge University in 2011. His belief in my work and support first as my thesis supervisor and now as my mentor, editor, advisor, and cheerleader, played a key role. His deep insights, understanding of the subject, and advice have been immeasurable.

Thank you to the two reviewers, my niece Shenara Fernando and Dr Huong Dam, for their patient editorial input and advice almost one to two years back. To the team at Partridge Singapore - Jade Bailey and Editor Dana Dyer Pierson - for their patience and belief.

Thank you, Dr Pete Ooi, for inviting me to teach the subject at the European Business School MBA and DBA programmes from 2013 and for contributing a message.

In terms of the book itself, whilst the above-mentioned played a key role, so too did my professors at the INSEAD Business school in France. Professor Ludo Van Der Heyden first gave me the opportunity to be on the faculty in the INSEAD Advanced Management Program between 2005 and 2011 on seeing the sustainable value I had created for an apparel manufacturer in the realm of social sustainability. Professor Jonathan Story believed in the potential of sustainability-led differentiation and, along with Noshua Watson, wrote the first case on women go beyond, followed by Professor Amitava Chattopadhyay, who wrote the second case.

Thanks to Professor Marc Le Menestrel for his continuous encouragement regarding my belief in the subject of strategic corporate sustainability and for inviting me to teach it at the Universiti of Pompeu Fabra in Spain. Thank you, Professor Jens Meyer of CEDEP, for the opportunity to teach the subject at the Managing Business Excellence Program in China. Thanks to Professor Luk Van Wassenhove for inviting me to be an executive in residence at the INSEAD Business School Social Innovation Centre from September 2010 and exposing me to global best practices of businesses committed to walk the talk, and for inviting me to be his co-author on an INSEAD case and collaborating on more than seven INSEAD case studies of sustainable initiatives the centre developed with Professor Mark Hunter.

My thanks to Prof Renée Mauborgne, whom I first met in 2007 at the World Strategy Summit and who thereafter became a major source of inspiration the past eight years on every initiative I had championed, along with Professor W Chan Kim of Blue Ocean Strategy fame and the team at the Malaysia Blue Ocean Strategy Institute, led by Dr Park, who challenged me to excellence in all I did.

At Cambridge University Institute of Sustainable Leadership, the excellent faculty at the post-graduate certificate in sustainable business and master's in studies course between 2007 and 2014 included Dr Theo Hacking, Dr Wayne Visser, Michael Wright, David Rice and a host of brilliant and inspirational faculty and administrators. Thank you.

ILLUSTRATIONS

CHAPTER 1

The Reality
Global Sustainability Challenges

1.1 A Wake-Up Call!

The nominal global world product growth has quadrupled in the past thirty years, from around US$22.4 trillion in 1985 to over US$90 trillion in 2015.[9]

Nations and businesses have exploited and converted the planet's limited resources to products and services at an unprecedented rate, with little thought to the need for its regeneration. Meanwhile, global debt rose from US$87 trillion in 2000 to an estimated US$199 trillion by 2014[10] alongside mountains of waste in this age of irresponsible consumption. The projected nominal global world product by 2020 is US$133 trillion forecasted to reach US$308 trillion by 2030.[11] *This level of growth is unsustainable. No less than two to three planets will be required to meet this level of resource utilisation.*

The unabated growth of the global population from 7 billion in 2015 projected to reach 9 billion by 2050, with more than 70 per cent living in the water-stressed, polluted Southern Hemisphere, will require water to survive.

---

9   Global GDP projections - standard chartered research, 2010.
10 'Global Debt', *Financial Times*, 5 February 2015.
11 Global GDP projections - standard chartered research, 2010.

The direct impact of fresh-water scarcity on agriculture, which today consumes over 68 per cent of this resource, will lead to global water and food shortages never experienced before. In addition, the hydroelectricity-generating water reservoirs will be at risk as the rainwater cycle (hydrological cycle) is affected. Globally, 68 per cent of electricity generation is fossil-fuel dependent, with coal 41 per cent, gas 22 per cent, and oil 5 per cent as of 2013.[12] The current fossil-fuel-driven global economy directly impacts climate change due to carbon emissions, which cause global warming.

The pace of conversion to green energy sources is unlikely to outpace the evolving crises to give the planet a chance of surviving the impacts of the past thirty years of growth at any cost. This confirms the need for a step change towards the aggressive induction of green energy and technology to reduce carbon emissions.

The reality is that global warming has nearly reached +2 degrees Celsius and is moving towards +4 degrees Celsius in the medium term. The catastrophic impact of this in terms of sea-level rise projected to increase twenty feet (six metres) will significantly affect the following nations: China, Vietnam, India, Indonesia, Bangladesh, Japan, the United States, Egypt, Brazil, the Netherlands, the Philippines, Thailand, Myanmar, Nigeria, the United Kingdom, Mexico, Italy, Germany, Malaysia, and France more than others. Between 2 per cent and 62 per cent of the national populations will be impacted, with 3 million to 85 million

---

[12] 'Crude Crash Holds Back Shift to Renewables', *Financial Times*, 14 July 2015.

affected. China, Vietnam, India, Indonesia, and Bangladesh are the top five nations to be affected, with close to 211 million in harm's way. Additionally, 62 per cent of the population of the Netherlands is also estimated to be affected.[13]

Climate-related health issues will impact all of humanity, as recently reported in *The Lancet* medical journal of 23 June 2015, which refers to climate change as a medical emergency which demands an emergency response and confirms fossil fuels are killing humanity.[14] Drought, heat waves (which caused more than three thousand deaths in India and Pakistan in June 2015), and floods will cause massive displacement and environmental migration.

Most of the world's 7 billion population and future generations will suffer the consequences of global warming, water scarcity, and air pollution due to the lack of urgency amongst global leaders to enforce legislation to exit polluting industries, fossil-fuel-guzzling vehicles, and coal-powered energy.

The most startling fact is that despite all the scientific evidence, governments continue to subsidise fossil fuels to the tune of US$5.3 trillion per annum and deforestation at US$1.1 trillion per annum in the name of economic development and GDP growth. This is despite the fact that both these factors are major

---

[13] B. Strauss, 'Coastal Nations, Megacities Face 20 Feet of Sea Rise', *Climate Central*, 9 July 2015.
[14] 'Health and Climate Change: Policy Responses to Protect Public Health', *The Lancet* medical journal, 23 June 2015.

causes of catastrophic global warming.[15] *In reality, governments are accelerating global warming by doing so.*

Today, consumers waste between 30 and 40 per cent of all agricultural produce and processed food, creating mountains of waste. This is one of the many other challenges the planet is set to face. Deforestation directly impacts ecosystems and biodiversity with more than 52 per cent of the planet's species already extinct due to decimating 50 per cent of global forest cover.[16]

A breath of clean air, a glass of fresh water, and the chance to experience nature could soon be a luxury within the reach of only a few. What nation can achieve GDP growth and what business can succeed without water? Can humanity survive without fresh water and clean air? Global water scarcity is set to reach a crisis point by 2025. Will a breath of clean air soon be a rare commodity in the two most populous nations on the planet? If these two factors don't energise all of humanity to urgent action for sustainability, what will?

1.2 What Happened Since Rio, 1992-2015?

Since the Earth Summit in Rio in 1992, the planet's **carbon emissions** moved up from less than twenty-one gigatons in 1992 to around thirty-two gigatons in 2014,[17] whilst carbon concentrations in the atmosphere moved up from under two hundred fifty parts per million in 1992 to four hundred parts per million in March

---

[15] IMF, June 2015.

[16] 'Cover Decline by 50% in Past 30 Years and 52% of Animal Species in Past 40 Years', *Yale Environment e360 Digest 2014 - Global Forest* (2014).

[17] 'Source IAEA', *Financial Times,* 13 March 2015.

2015, according to NASA.[18] Also, 2014 was designated the warmest year ever recorded on the planet, and the first few months of 2015 were warmer than the corresponding months in 2014. Every ensuing year from now is poised to be warmer than the one before. The global obsession for fossil fuels, which accounts for 68 per cent of global electricity generation and more than 90 per cent of transportation, is the major contributor.[19]

What impact have the accords, initiatives, declarations, commitments, resolutions, and protocols had to date towards exiting fossil fuels and creating a more sustainable world? Instead, we have global leaders who subsidise this obsession. The unabated growth of carbon emissions during the past twenty-two years points in the direction of a *catastrophic global leadership failure*! National and business leaders responsible for the utilisation of the planet's resources have done so with little or no regard to the strategic impact of their decisions.

Economic growth (GDP) and profitability have been the only goals pursued by nations and businesses. Whilst the needs of a few have been excessively met, at present, inequality is rampant, and the needs of future generations have been significantly compromised. The recent IAEA figures indicate that CO_2 emissions stayed the same in 2013 and 2014 at 32 gigatons for the first time in forty years, despite a 3 per cent global economic growth. However, the fact remains they have grown year on year, and the planet has been in an environmental coma, deteriorating for forty years consecutively, already suffering irreparable damage. Whilst

---

[18]   NASA – National Aeronautics and Space Administration, USA, March 2015.
[19]   'Crude Crash Holds Back Shift to Renewables', *Financial Times*, 14 July 2015.

a year of stabilisation is a ray of hope, one cannot avoid the fact that 2014 was the hottest year on record, with 2015 set to beat it.

CO_2 concentrations reached 400 ppm. Rising sea levels projected to get to twenty feet (six metres), with global warming set to pass two degrees Celsius, will threaten supply chains and affect humanity as never before.

Social inequality is more pronounced than ever, with the concentration of global wealth among eighty-five individuals with more wealth than half the world's population.[20] This is the reason we have a global 99 per cent movement. The richest 1 per cent needs to be more accountable and use its wealth for good with urgency.

1.3 The Rising Influence of Business

The rising influence of business in the global economy is confirmed by the fact that by 2011, business occupied over 40 per cent of the top one hundred global economic entity[21] positions, usurping nations. If this trend continues, by 2030 we could see 70 to 80 per cent of the top one hundred global economic entities being businesses.

This highlights the increasing influence of business and the urgent need for business leaders to be engaged in addressing global sustainability challenges. It brings to focus the diminishing control and influence of nations to impact global sustainability and the corresponding rise of business. The concentration of business

---

20   'Debate Global Inequality', *FT Wealth,* Summer, 2014, pp. 40-41.
21   'UN Global Compact Sri Lanka Analysis', *Top 100 Global Economic Entities Dec. 2012* (2011).

influence is highlighted by Professor Robert Eccles's research, which reveals that just one thousand business entities account for more than 50 per cent of the market value of the sixty thousand publicly traded companies, and they virtually control the global economy. Just eighty-three companies account for 33 per cent of the US$32 trillion combined revenue.[22]

Since 1980, the number of climate-change-induced disasters per annum has risen from an average 80–120 to between 350–450 in the past decade.

The cost of devastation is estimated to be US$300 billion[23] per annum. The cost of environmental impacts on global business went up from US$2.5 trillion in 2009 to nearly US$3.0 trillion[24] in 2013, confirming that business performance has been significantly affected and that the best-laid plans could be thwarted by sustainability-related risks.

As John Elkington of triple bottom line[25] fame says, 'Few companies have taken the next step of concrete action for making the transition to the new paradigm.' The present UN secretary general, Ban Ki Moon, captured the reality when he said, 'Our current economic mindset and models increasingly look like a global

---

[22]   http://www.bloomberg.com/news/2012-09-11/top1000-companies-weild-power-reserved-for-nations.html.

[23]   'Outlook on the Global Agenda 2015', World Economic Forum Global Agenda Councils, pp. 26–28.

[24]   L. Hepler and B. Grady, 'Environment as Economic Threat: How Sustainability Defines Risk', February 4, 2015.

[25]   J. Elkington, *Cannibals with Forks*, Best Business Books, 2014.

suicide pact, we mined our way to growth, we burned our way to prosperity. We believe in consumption without consequences.'[26]

1.4 Halt Deforestation in 2030 or Now?

Disregard for 'natural capital' is the operating paradigm. Governments and businesses currently perceive that all natural resources must be exploited to propel growth. It has been a question of how and when this resource can be utilised and never about the need for conservation or regeneration. This attitude has resulted in the planet losing more than 50 per cent of its forest cover and 52 per cent of animal species in the past thirty to forty years[27] – a catastrophic level of natural resource exploitation! Forests provide 75 per cent of fresh water; therefore, we have significantly compromised this resource and the rainwater cycle.

Is it any surprise that we will have global water scarcity by 2025? This has directly contributed to a warmer planet, as the green cover that has absorbed CO_2 and the warmth of the sun's rays is no longer around to do so.

The recent Global Canopy Programme Forest 500's 2015 report[28] highlights that just five hundred companies, organisations, nations, and individuals are responsible for global deforestation. This is made up of 250 companies with combined revenues of US$4.5 trillion, of which only *six companies* had policies to protect forests; 150 investors and lenders; 50 nations; and 50 other organisations

---

26   http://www.un.org/news/press/docs/2011/sgsm13372.doc.htm.
27   'Cover Decline by 50% in Past 30 Years and 52% of Animal Species in Past 40 Years', *Yale Environment e360 Digest 2014 - Global Forest* (2014).
28   Global canopy program Forest 500-2015 report (http://www.globalcanopy.org)

that control global supply chains for commodities. These five hundred organisations have been directly responsible for the accelerated decimation of forests to grow commodities. The key forest-risk commodities, such as soya, palm oil, beef, leather, timber, paper, and pulp with government subsidised resource extraction of around US$1.1 trillion in 2011, is the major reason for this crisis.[29]

The key nations that have the remaining rainforests are decimating them. In the Amazon basin, deforestation subsidises timber, soya, and beef; the Congo basin does the same for timber; and Southeast Asia for palm oil, timber, pulp, and paper.

Today, the lack of awareness and appreciation of a nation's natural capital and the ignorance of the impacts of unsustainable deforestation by most national leaders have contributed to the absence of sustainable policies and controls to curb the decimation of forest cover. Instead, government subsidies encourage rapid deforestation in the name of development. National governments contribute to accelerated climate change by subsidising fossil fuel and deforestation to the tune of US$6-8 billion per annum. Brazil controlled deforestation during 2004 to 2012, but ironically, since the introduction of the new forest code in 2014, increased deforestation of the Amazon (Earth Lung) is happening at an unprecedented rate. The same is true in the Congo and Indonesia. Indonesian forest fires in August and September 2015 confirm this.

---

[29] Burger. A 'How Government Subsidies Drive Deforestation and Inequality' Triple Pundit 6th April 2015 from a working paper titled 'Subsidies to key commodities driving forest loss-Implications for private climate finance - Will McFarland, Shelagh Whitley and Gabrielle Kissinger March 2015

On 23 September 2014, the UN Climate Summit launched the 'New York Declaration on Forests', which made a commitment to cut the rate of deforestation by 50 per cent by 2020 and halt it by 2030. If Brazil's deforestation is an indication of what's happening, can we wait till 2030? By 2044, will we have any forest cover left?

1.5 Do We Take Fresh Water for Granted?

Are businesses and nations taking clean, fresh water for granted, assuming they will have access to this life-sustaining resource despite the looming water scarcity after 2025? If one studies the make-up of the 3 per cent of fresh water the planet holds, 2.5 per cent is located in glaciers, groundwater, and permafrost. In terms of the groundwater stored in the Earth's thirty-seven largest aquifers, twenty-one have exceeded the sustainability tipping point, and thirteen are significantly stressed.[30] The surface and atmosphere hold the balance 0.5 per cent in the form of freshwater lakes, soil moisture, atmosphere, wetlands, rivers, and vegetation. We use 68 per cent of the freshwater for agriculture. Over 40 per cent is used just to produce the crops; domestic and other industrial users account for 19 per cent. Power-generation plants take 10 per cent, and 3 per cent evaporates from reservoirs.[31] Global warming is accelerating melting of the polar caps and sea-level rise.

The imminent drilling of the Arctic by Shell shows the paucity of strategic thinking on the planet today. Can any business operate

---

[30]   UCI led study using NASA data 2003-2013 UC Irvine/NASA/JPL-Caltech
[31]   Global Water security - Intelligence community assessment ICA 2012-08, 2 February 2012

without water? Can any nation survive without water? Can humanity survive without clean, fresh water?

Unlike at any time in history, fresh water will be the scarcest and most precious resource in the next decade. The limited fresh water available has been polluted, confirming the inconvenient truth that we have failed to protect our fresh-water resources or harvest the rainwater. The changing hydrological cycle, due to climate change and the decimation of forests, is already causing severe floods and unprecedented droughts in many nations today. The looming global water scarcity predicted to cause both physical and economic water shortages by 2025 will significantly impact over 70 per cent of the world's population currently living in the Southern Hemisphere.

Meanwhile, global headlines confirm that nation after nation is experiencing the impacts of climate change, with extreme weather conditions causing havoc to humanity. The impending crisis the planet is faced with will cause displacement, and a new category of migrants will take centre stage: *environmental migrants*. They will migrate from Southern Hemisphere nations to the water-rich Northern Hemisphere.

This pace of resource utilisation due to the insatiable appetites of nations and business to exploit natural resources in the past thirty years has left resources no time to regenerate. In the case of water, we have polluted groundwater and aquifers in the name of manufacture. Toxic residues from fertiliser leach into rivers and groundwater, causing major health risks to rural agricultural communities.

Figure 1. World Resources Institute Water Stress Map
Source: WRI Aqueduct aqueduct.wri.org

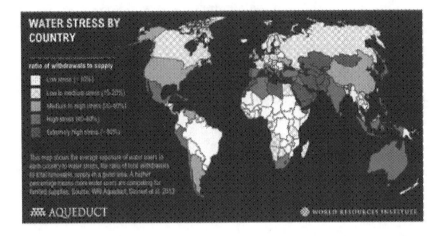

Both physical and economic water shortages will threaten the very basis of human life by 2025.[32] The water-scarcity map makes it clear as to why twenty-first-century global conflicts will revolve around access to the planet's 3 per cent of fresh water. Today, many of the global tension points relate to access to this precious life-giving resource. Syria and many African, Asian, and Middle Eastern nations are proof of this fact.

The forecast is that Southern Hemisphere regions like Asia Pacific, Sub-Saharan Africa, the Middle East, and North Africa are the most vulnerable.

Many of them are already experiencing either physical or economic water shortages today, and the issue will reach a crisis point by 2025.

---

[32] World Resources Institute **Water Stress Map** "Source: WRI Aqueduct aqueduct. wri.org"

The OECD Environmental Outlook Report predicts that more than 5 billion people will suffer water shortages by 2030. The rapid pollution of all our waterways and groundwater will be a very big problem in Latin America, the Middle East, northern and Sub-Saharan Africa. Water scarcity will impact business both directly and indirectly, as agriculture and manufacture will require water as a key input, some industries more than others.

1.6 Do We Take Clean Air for Granted?

Coal-driven electricity and petroleum-based transportation generate the emissions that have contributed to crisis levels of air pollution, where the air-quality index (AQI) regularly reaches 60-100 ppm in many of the urban areas of the world. In key Chinese and Indian cities, the 100-300 ppm hazardous level is crossed 20 to 50 per cent of days. The resultant health risk has made living in many urban areas a challenge. New Delhi was named the most polluted city in the world in 2015. According to a recent survey, thirteen of the twenty most polluted global cities are now in India, overtaking China as the most polluted nation.[33] Air pollution is seen as the sixth most significant trend globally and third in Asia.[34] The documentary *Under the Dome*, developed by CCTV anchor Chai Jing in March 2015, gives a detailed account of the issues in China and the current health crisis.

The level of toxic air pollution is exacerbated by the increasing number of automobiles and diesel transport vehicles, as well as by increased coal-powered energy and air travel globally. In the

---

[33] Economist February 17, 2015 - Pollution - The Cost of Clean Air
[34] World Economic Forum global agenda councils 'Outlook on the global agenda 2015 pg 23

United States, four out of every ten people live in areas with unhealthy ozone levels. Cities like London, Paris, Seoul, Kuala Lumpur, Bangkok, Jakarta, and Singapore all experience unhealthy levels of smog.

The cross-border migration of industrial pollution of EU nations, Chinese and Indonesian forest-fire pollution are causing major health issues in bordering nations. A majority of city dwellers in the developing world are experiencing a significant increase of upper-respiratory-tract infections, asthma, and a host of lung diseases.[35]

If we continue this way, 'a breath of fresh air' will increasingly be a challenge for 99 per cent of humanity. Oxygen canisters and cafes and high-tech facemasks will soon be the norm in most of the polluted cities of the world for that elusive breath. This will be exacerbated when 66 per cent of the world's population migrates to urban areas by 2050.

1.7 Is There a Glimmer of Hope?

On 23 September 2014, the UN Climate Summit launched the New York Declaration on Forests to halt deforestation by 2030. At the current rates of decimation, 75 per cent of global forest cover would have been decimated by then. On 2 November 2014, 194 nations agreed with the conclusions of IPCC scientists on climate risks, but how is it that most of them don't have a national sustainability strategy to address the crisis? Only thirty to forty nations have one today.

---

[35] Lancet Medical Journal 23 June 2015, Health and Climate change :Policy responses to protect public health

On 12 November 2014, the leaders of the United States and China, nations accounting for more than 32 per cent of global carbon emissions in 2013, announced significant commitments.

US president Barack Obama committed to reduce US carbon pollution by between 26 and 28 per cent below 2005 levels by 2025. The Chinese premier, Xi Jinping, pledged to get 20 per cent of the country's power and energy from zero-carbon sources by 2030.

The question is, will the Republican Party leaders who oppose even the use of the term 'climate change' in the United States and rising demand for energy in China derail these commitments? In the past thirty years, we have seen unprecedented degradation of the planet in the name of GDP growth and business performance. Will this change? A recent report confirmed that China needs to invest 6.5 per cent of GDP to clean up the debilitating environmental pollution.[36]

All nations that delay sustainability policy and strategy implementation to pursue economic growth will have to pay the cost of cleanup for the delay, as is the case with China and India. The absence of an economic reward system that recognises both business and governments for their commitment to sustainability exacerbates the issue. Nations like Australia and Canada are undoing many sustainability initiatives of the past, demonstrating how climate-denying leaders can drag nations back to prehistoric times simply to sell fossil fuels. The EU is under pressure from industry

---

[36] Crane.K & Mao.Z (2015), Costs of selected policies to address Air Pollution in China © 2015 Rand Corporation

to water down the bold regulations initiated. Governments keep sinking funds into fossil-fuel subsidies, and the oil-industry lobby keeps delaying key legislation that can accelerate the move to renewable energy. The recent decline in oil prices has helped the non-oil-producing nations to reduce subsidies, but are they using the funds to invest in renewable energy for the nation's future?

The emerging silver lining is a new breed of sustainability mindset leaders of nations and businesses such as presidents Barack Obama and Xi Jinping, Pope Francis, Jeff Immelt of GE, Paul Polman of Unilever, Elon Musk of Tesla, and organisations like Google, Apple, Toyota, Puma, Nike, Patagonia, IKEA, Marks & Spencer (M&S), Wal-Mart; nations like Costa Rica, Denmark, Sweden, the United Kingdom, Singapore, and South Korea; and key influencers like John Elkington, Al Gore, David Suzuki, Jeffery Sachs, and Nicholas Stern.

1.8 False Beliefs and Hopes of Leaders?

Global inaction and lack of urgency to address the challenges the world is faced with seem to be a result of many false beliefs and hopes amongst leaders of nations and businesses. Pope Francis captured the reality recently in the 192-page *Laudato Si*, as reported in the *Financial Times* of 17 and 19 June 2015, where he fairly and squarely laid blame on business leaders and politicians when he said, 'The idea of infinite or unlimited growth, which proves so attractive to economists, financiers, and experts in technology **is** based on the lie that there is an infinite supply of the earth's goods, and this leads to the planet being squeezed dry beyond every limit."[37]

World leaders procrastinate decisions in the belief that
- science will find a way
- scientists are exaggerating the forecasts
- we need to address more pressing issues
- our focus and priority is surviving today
- we must thrive before future generations.

The current global order is flawed, and the following assumptions perpetuate it. Many global leaders act and behave as though they do believe the assumptions to be true or have irresponsibly convinced themselves to justify inaction or apathy. This is the reality.

1. The global economy can grow perpetually and utilise all resources.
2. Resources will regenerate themselves.
3. Short-termism needs to guide all decisions.
4. National leaders must focus on winning the next election.
5. Corporate leaders must focus on quarterly profits.
6. The global system only rewards the short term.
7. The disproportionate influence of nations and large MNCs is ok.
8. The incentive for the wealthiest to get even wealthier is ok.
9. 'Natural capital' is a limitless resource

---

[37] Financial Times 19 June 2015 'Pope says multinationals and greed threaten environment'

10. The exploitation of disadvantaged women and children is ok.
11. The exploitation of a nation's natural resources by other nations, with little benefit to the nations whose birthright it was is ok.

The prevailing level of inaction and lack of urgency to face up to the reality of catastrophic impacts of water scarcity, polluted air, and rapid deforestation cannot be explained. Today, the world leaders calling for urgent action on climate change are the same ones who invest between US$6-8 trillion dollars on subsidising fossil fuels and deforestation.

1.9 A Call for Urgent Action!

A BBC news item on 28 January 2015 titled 'The World Can Cut Carbon Emissions and Live Well' said 'Forests around the world will need to be expanded by 5-15 per cent to limit global temperature rises to 2 degrees Celsius, and crop yields must rise by 40-60 per cent, and there would need to be hundreds of millions of electric cars on the road by 2050.' It refers to the need for CO_2 emitted per unit of electricity to fall by 90 per cent, along with the other conditions, if the planet was to prevent the +2 degree Celsius rise. The project is led by the UK Department of Energy, Climate Change (DECC), using the global calculator to develop models of the world's energy, land, and food systems.

Business urgently needs to wake up to the reality of operating in a water-constrained world and ask the tough questions regarding its current product range: Is this the best use of scarce water resources for the planet? Businesses and nations will need to review water as a key supply-chain risk, as water shortages will impact its sourcing strategy. Incorporating water-risk calculations using the Ecolab Water Risk Monetiser will need to be an integral part of all sustainability-risk audits.

How will humanity cope with this crisis? Will we see *environmental migration* at an unprecedented rate? How must national and business leaders address this life-threatening issue with urgency? Fresh-water management has to be a joint priority for a sustainable planet with renewable energy. Future risk mitigation requires business investment to secure access to water by 2025, when the projected water crisis unfolds. Multinational corporations like Unilever, Nestle, and General Mills are amongst those most sensitive to this business risk and have set strategies in motion to manage the risk by significantly reducing their water footprint.

Nations will need to exit fossil fuels and scale up the investment in green energy for 100 per cent of their energy needs. Nations like Spain, Denmark, Costa Rica, and many EU countries have set the pace. China and the United States have acknowledged the climate crisis and are taking decisive action to manage its impact.

More than one hundred nations have set renewable-energy targets, which need to be translated to action with urgency. As a first step, the fossil-fuel subsidies need to be rechanneled to invest in renewable energy. As an intermediary step, exiting coal and moving to natural gas will reduce carbon emissions. Enlightened business is also taking the lead and moving to secure 100 per cent of its energy requirements with 'green energy'. The 100% Club in the United States is one such initiative, with Intel, IKEA, Mars, along with Apple and Google investing to secure 100 per cent renewable energy. Unfortunately, the enlightened nations and businesses are few and far between.

The world needs to dramatically scale up renewable energy to move from 22 per cent in 2014 to over 80 per cent of energy needs by 2030, halt deforestation, and reforest. Businesses and nations must halt *deforestation* today and invest in *reforestation* and the *preservation of forest cover.* Enlightened businesses will need to invest in reforestation with urgency, as Unilever and WWF have done with the recent announcement to protect one million trees in Brazil and Indonesia.[38] Enlightened nations need to halt deforestation and jointly invest in reforestation in partnership with business; for example, all businesses in the tourism sector could be inspired to do so. Forests and green cover are designed to be the Earth's lung for humanity. The current decimation of forest cover to achieve GDP growth and supposedly development has paid no attention to regeneration or replacement. The world needs to wake up to the urgent need to preserve what's left, especially in the remaining rainforests – the Amazon, Congo, and Borneo – to preserve the 'Earth lung' and keep global warming in check and the hydrological cycle uninterrupted.

Businesses can play a planet-saving role where national leaders have failed, provided triple-bottom-line thinking guides and influences every business decision. A change in paradigm from creating *short-term shareholder value to strategic sustainable*

---

[38]   Edie.net 8 July 2015 Matt Field : WWF and Unilever announce campaign to protect one million trees

value will need to pervade all business. The rising tide of influence makes it imperative that business leaders (CEOs, boards, C-suites) have sustainability mindsets for the stewardship of the planet's limited resources. Managing both the present and the future in a responsible way will never happen unless we have leaders with sustainability mindsets. A new approach that leads to *urgent action for a sustainable planet* needs to be the focus of all business leaders and governments. An enlightened public-private partnership that focuses on urgent action for the planet is needed today.

Nations and businesses have saved up trillions of dollars in cash reserves and wealth funds for future investment. Today, the survival of the planet is at risk. This fact demands an unleashing of these cash reserves to invest in renewable energy to mitigate the risk of global warming. The one thousand largest listed companies that account for 50 per cent of market capitalisation; the ninety large, polluting companies that account for over 63 per cent of global pollution; and the five hundred organisations and individuals that drive deforestation urgently have to change and invest in green technology, exit fossil fuels, and mainstream sustainability with urgency.

A systemic change in which sustainable consumption and sustainable resource utilisation drive all national, corporate, and individual decisions must replace the current paradigm.

As Per Espen Stoknes, a Norwegian psychologist, has suggested:

> Climate change is an opportunity for economic development – an entire energy system has to be

redesigned from the wastefulness of the previous century to a much smarter mode of doing things. It's a great opportunity to improve global collaboration and knowledge sharing and to create a more just society. So climate change is a fantastic opportunity to encourage our global humanity to emerge. We need to be talking about this.[39]

The next few chapters outline why business action is the best hope for the planet. Chapter 2, The Reality outlines the business response to date. We move to strategic solutions in chapter 3, 'The Challenge'. In chapter 4, 'The Opportunity', the need for adopting strategic corporate sustainability and mobilising the 7 Imperatives for Sustainable Business is outlined. In chapter 5, 'The Future', a direct and urgent call for action is outlined with initiatives to proactively impact the emerging sustainability challenges from the perspective of business and nations.

---

[39] Schiffman.R, Environment 360 July 9th 2015, How can we make people care about climate change?

CHAPTER 2

The Reality
Corporate Response
to Sustainability Challenges

2.1 What Corporate Leaders Say and Do in Reality

UN Secretary General Kofi Anan set up the UN Global Compact in 1999[40] to engage business in the pursuit of a sustainable world. The ten principles,[41] covering human rights, labour, environment, and anti-corruption, along with the corporate-sustainability blueprint, challenged business to internalise sustainability and communicate on its progress (COP).

Between 2000 and 2013, the UN Global Compact had 11,286 chairmen and chief executive officers of companies make a commitment to the ten UNGC principles[42] for companies to deliver long-term value in financial, social, environmental, and ethical terms.[43]

However, 4,086 (36.2 per cent) were delisted for not submitting Communication on Progress reports. This is the reality, where many businesses commit to pursue sustainability, but in reality 40-50 per cent just pay lip service. Today, the UN Global Compact has around 12,000 signatories from 145 nations, of which around

---

[40] UN Global Compact-*https://www.unglobalcompact.org*
[41] Refer Appendix 4 – UN Global compact principles
[42] UNGC 10 Principles- *https://www.unglobalcompact.org*
[43] UNGC Corporate blue print *https://www.unglobalcompact.org*

8,000 are business entities that can be a force for good. However, it takes sustainability mindset leadership to transition from words to action.

The 2013 UN Global Compact-Accenture CEO Study,[44] in its executive summary, highlights that:

> 67% of respondents **'do not believe'** that business is doing enough to address global sustainability. It also states that **business efforts on sustainability may have reached a plateau** with many business leaders expressing doubts about the pace of change and the scale of their impact. Of the sample only 33% reported sustainability impacts that business is making sufficient efforts to address global sustainability challenges. 37% see the lack of a link to business value as a barrier to accelerating progress and that **sustainability continues to be pigeonholed as a marginal issue**, still regarded by many companies as an extra cost to be cut in the face of short-term financial pressures.

The UNGC/Accenture Survey in 2010[45] reported that of the 766 UNGC signatory company CEOs interviewed, 93 per cent believed sustainability issues will be critical to the future; 96 per cent of CEOs believed that sustainability issues should be fully integrated into strategy and operations, but fewer than 30 per cent did so.

---

[44]   UN Global compact Accenture CEO survey(2013)'Architects of a Better World'

[45]   UN Global Compact Accenture CEO survey 2010 pp.12

The UN Global Compact-Accenture CEO Study - Sustainability 2013 Architects of a Better World[46] further highlights that by industry, CEOs seem to feel that sustainability is less important, down from 62 per cent to 43 per cent in automotive; from 63 per cent to 53 per cent in consumer goods; from 68 per cent to 59 per cent in the energy industry; and from 68 per cent to 61 per cent in the utilities sector.

The UNGC Accenture CEO Studies in 2010 and 2013 and surveys conducted by McKinsey in 2011[47] and 2014, the 2011 KPMG/EIU Report[48] all had over 90 per cent of CEOs make commitments to embed sustainability in corporate strategy, but in reality, only between 20 and 30 per cent did so. In the McKinsey Survey in February 2014,[49] only *13 per cent* of CEOs considered sustainability as the most important priority, which means 87 per cent didn't. The bottom line is all the surveys conducted confirm *a gap between narrative commitments and implementation reality.* The question is, how do we bring about the needed transformation? Though the scientific evidence overwhelmingly confirms the emerging threat of climate change, when a CEO or national leader sits on the hot seat, the 'knowing-doing gap' widens as many short-term fires need to be put out.

An exploratory study was conducted in 2013-14 as an integral part of my Cambridge studies, to establish what conditions enable business to mobilise and embed sustainability in corporate strategy. A UN Global Compact local network representative of the key

---

46   UN Global compact Accenture CEO survey 2013 results
47   Mckinsey (2011) The Business of sustainability
48   KPMG/EIU(2011) Corporate Sustainability a progress report
49   Mckinsey(2014) global survey results February 2014

challenges and profile of a majority of the one hundred-odd local networks was selected. The network had forty UNGC signatory companies with over five hundred affiliates and subsidiaries. The network was rated as being among the top ten local networks globally in 2013 and won the Asia Pacific best network peer award in 2009, because of its innovative approaches to embedding sustainability in corporate strategy. The focus of the study was to understand the current inhibitions, practices, and attitudes towards sustainability and what conditions were specifically mobilised by business to mainstream sustainability in corporate strategy. The following are my key findings.

- It highlighted beyond reasonable doubt that business leaders perceived that sustainability and CSR are the same, as a majority of them had never been exposed to the subject in business schools.
- There is a perception among CEOs/boards that pursuing sustainability was a high cost that needed major changes to business as usual.
- There is a flawed assumption that all organisations that sign up to the UN Global Compact embed sustainability in corporate strategy. This fact necessitates an approach where all signatories need 'high engagement' in the first one to two years to help them do so.
- In most cases, the business had two distinct strategies: a corporate strategy that got most of the focus/investment and a separate low-priority CSR/sustainability strategy.
- The CSR initiatives were primarily for achieving publicity and PR.

- Wherever the leader and board were committed to sustainability, the business mainstreamed sustainability in corporate strategy.
- The common factor amongst 'high-sustainability' conglomerates was that the CEO/managing director/ chairman personally led the embedding of sustainability in corporate strategy because of a conviction of the need for doing so.
- They 'positioned and framed' sustainability as a corporate growth strategy and ensured a corporate governance structure to do so.
- Embedding sustainability in corporate strategy was the first step.
- The forward-thinking and most successful conglomerates moved to a second step of 'sustainability-led differentiation and innovation'.
- They linked compensation and rewards to sustainability performance and were committed to sustainability reporting.

The above key findings were validated in terms of the best practice of global sustainability leaders, existing literature, and in turn laid the foundation for the 7 Imperatives for Sustainable Business outlined in chapter 4. I realised that the seven key imperatives could be mobilised by organisations pursing sustainable business if more CEOs and boards were made aware of them. I believe this is the way to energise organisations to follow the path of strategic corporate sustainability.

2.2 Sustainability Measurement and Reporting

A review of the top 500 US S&P Index[50] companies and the 1,600 MSCI World Index[51] companies in 24 developed markets revealed that carbon emissions over the period 2008 to 2012 increased from 14,863 metric tons to 14,990 metric tons, as per the State of Green Biz Business report in 2014; the same is true of water use and solid-waste disclosure.[52]

The 2014 survey by Corporate Knights Capital of the 4,609 largest companies listed in stock exchanges confirms that *97 per cent of companies are failing to report on the full set of 'first-generation sustainability indicators'* such as GHG, waste, water, etc., with over 75 per cent not transparent on water consumption[53]; only 3 per cent or 128 did. Sustainable business needs to minimise their carbon, water, and ecological footprints; stop polluting; halt deforestation; and minimise waste. To do so, businesses must start by committing to measurement and transparency.

The Carbon Disclosure Project has around five thousand companies in 2014.[54] Ninety per cent of reporting companies had data on electricity and GHG emissions, but only 10 per cent reported on water. The bottom line is that while global emissions of business have increased, 97 per cent of the world's largest

---

50   Standard and Poor Index - *us.spindices.com/indices/equity/sp-500*
51   Morgan Stanley Corporate Index -*www.msci.com/resources/factsheets/ index_fact.../msci-world-index.pdf*
52   Globescan and Trucost (2014) - Green biz state of green business
53   Confino .J (2014) 19 October 2014 - Finance hub from Guardian Sustainable Business
54   Lux Research - Corporate Sustainability Initiatives lack critical Data and Analytics April 7 2015

businesses don't consider it important enough to measure and report its sustainability impacts and resource utilisation.

2.3 Lack of Global Leadership

The World Economic Forum in 2015 identified *lack of global leadership* as one of the top ten global trends.[55] Eighty-six per cent of all respondents to the global agenda agree that we have a leadership crisis in the world today. The key skills identified in the World Economic Forum report were global perspective, collaboration, consensus-building, and communication.

Pope Francis, in the encyclical *Laudato Si*, refers to the lack of global leadership and the nefarious role of 'economic powers', speculators, and financial markets that have caused the current climate crisis and calls for urgent moves to drastically cut carbon emissions, as scientific evidence clearly suggests global warming is mainly a result of human activity.[56]

Today, a handful of national and business leaders have a global perspective on the emerging sustainability challenges. Most lack the required urgency for sustainability-driven leadership because of the lack of exposure and education on the subject. As a result of this lack of appreciation of climate science, coupled with the 'short-termism trap', leaders have resorted to cosmetic actions and initiatives regarding sustainability, and the majority have decided to ignore the impending crisis.

---

[55] World Economic Forum global agenda councils 'Outlook on the global agenda 2015 pg 14-16, pg 52-63

[56] Financial Times 17 June 2015 'Pope takes climate to papacy's heart

The lack of consensus-building, collaboration, and communication for sustainability stems from the lack of engagement with the reality of climate change. Every leader endowed with the stewardship of either a nation or a business must preempt the impending catastrophe by facing up to reality. Unfortunately, most universities and business schools have failed to even remotely prepare them for this challenge.

2.4 How Prepared Are Corporate Leaders for Sustainability?

Many CEO survey results compiled by leading organisations between 2000 and 2013 give us an informed basis to make some assumptions of the level of preparedness of today's business leaders in terms of corporate sustainability leadership.

- Unprepared leaders – the majority, more than 90 per cent

The recent Corporate Knights survey (2014) of the 4,609 largest listed companies confirms that 97 per cent of the largest listed companies do not even report on first-generation key sustainability parameters.[57] The fact is that we have many leaders who are not sensitive to the need for sustainability as an issue. One has to bear in mind that 4,609 is a fraction of the companies listed in the world's stock exchanges. When you add the unlisted, family, small, and medium enterprises, the reality comes to light. Therefore, it would be safe to assume that the majority of business leaders of the world, in both listed and unlisted companies, would fall into this category.

---

[57]   Confino .J (2014) 19 October 2014 - Finance hub from Guardian Sustainable Business

'How concerned are CEOs about climate change? Not at all' was the heading of an article in the *Guardian* of 20 January 2015, referring to the Price Waterhouse Coopers eighteenth annual global CEO survey. Apparently, climate change did not even make it to the nineteen top risks CEOs prioritised for urgent action.[58] It goes on to state, 'It seems that CEOs are so overwhelmed by short-term fears that they are failing to look further ahead', bringing to focus the key issue of short-termism versus strategic decision-making.

Professor Jorgen Randers of the Norwegian Business School says, 'The capitalist system does not help, it is carefully designed to allocate capital to the most profitable projects and that is what we **don't** need today.'[59]

The 2013 MIT Sloan Management Review and Boston Consulting Group[60] study divided respondents appropriately to 'walkers and talkers' of sustainability, ninety organisations in each group. The study highlights that only 10 per cent say their companies fully tackle sustainability issues, with only 11 per cent ranking sustainability as a very significant issue. Only 9 per cent strongly agree that their companies are prepared for climate change, which means more than 90 per cent are not prepared for climate-change impacts and sustainability.

---

[58] Confino. J, The Guardian 20th January 2015
[59] Confino. J, The Guardian 20th January 2015
[60] MIT Sloan Management review (MIT SMR) and the Boston Consulting group (BCG) report December 2013 'Sustainability's Next frontier: Walking the Talk on the Sustainability issues that matter most'

This level of inaction and unpreparedness amongst business leaders to mainstream sustainability is not entirely their fault. The failure has to be attributed to business schools, which have failed to integrate the subject into their MBA curricula and as a result created a generation of C-suite leaders who are not schooled on the subject. The sad fact is that a handful of business schools do so even today. Therefore, the priority is to engage and inspire business schools to embrace the subject with urgency and create a new cadre of sustainability mindset leaders who are well prepared to straddle the new agenda.

- Reactive leaders – 7 per cent to 10 per cent at best

Many leaders are 'compliance-driven' in terms of sustainability and do the minimum that is required. They tend to react to sustainability crises as they occur. This approach does not place sustainability at the core of the business strategy. At best it is a 'bolt on CSR' approach. Phillip Kotler[61] referred to this as an attempt to 'Do good to look good'. Many business leaders assume that a CSR strategy is all that matters to convince their key public that they are a responsible and sustainable company. If one were to relate this to the available research on companies that have a CSR/sustainability report but have not embedded sustainability in corporate strategy, the figure would be around 7 to 10 per cent at best. The UN Global Compact, with around twelve thousand member organisations, of which roughly eight thousand are businesses, would be a good indication. The key point is that many business organisations, large and small, have

---

[61]   Kotler .P and Chang .N – Corporate social responsibility (2002)

joined the sustainability bandwagon more to be perceived as being responsible versus making sustainability central to their strategy.

- Integrated/aligned sustainability leaders – the enlightened 3 per cent

The World Business Council for Sustainable Development, the UN Global Compact LEAD programme, B-Corporation and the 100% Renewable Energy Club have sustainability mindset leaders who have understood the urgent need for sustainable business. The sustainability mindset leader will integrate sustainability strategy into corporate strategy. They are few and far between from over 500,000 business entities the world over.

The reality is that only around 3 per cent of the world's largest listed companies have committed to sustainability measurement and reporting. The silver lining is that some of the world leaders by industry are amongst them, e.g., Unilever, GE, Wal-Mart, Apple, and Toyota, where sustainability is the central and pivotal focus, which in turn influences all they do. They perceive sustainability as a business growth opportunity for creating sustainable value.

The 2013 MIT Sloan Management Review and Boston Consulting Group Report[62] suggest that 'Walkers' articulate a clear sustainability strategy, and 90 per cent of them have developed a sustainability strategy. Seventy per cent have placed sustainability permanently on their top management agenda; 50 per cent of

---

[62] MIT Sloan Management review (MIT SMR) and the Boston Consulting group (BCG) report Deemeber 2013 'Sustainability's Next frontier: Walking the Talk on the Sustainability issues that matter most'

walkers communicate and report on sustainability. The issue is that the 'walkers' are the minority worldwide.

2.5 Evolution of Sustainable Business

From the late 1960s, a philanthropist trait existed in every business leader, influenced by religious values. By the late 1980s, public relations and publicity took centre stage to position corporate social responsibility (CSR) or 'doing good to look good', as Drucker rightly called it. CSR can never be a substitute for integrated sustainability. The term 'sustainable development' emerged from the Bruntland Report 'Our Common Future', only in 1987 as a key new term that considered environmental and social implications of economic growth. In 1997, John Elkington coined the term 'triple bottom line' with his landmark book, *Cannibals with Forks*, and the need for economic, social, and environmental bottom lines to be considered with every decision. The concept is yet to be understood, and a great deal needs to be done before it is!

2.6 Business Schools and Sustainability

Climate change and the urgent need for preparing sustainability mindset leaders to respond to it has been ignored in most business schools. The majority of business schools in the world have *not* reinvented themselves by embracing the global sustainability agenda. They have not mainstreamed sustainability in MBA curricula or executive education. This has been a significant setback for creating sustainable mindset business leaders for the future. All business schools and universities need to recalibrate curricula to build sustainability leadership and triple-bottom-line mindsets with urgency. The core B-school subjects of operations, innovation, finance, strategy, marketing, and human-resource management need to have sustainability modules mainstreamed in the core curriculum to inspire and enlighten future leaders towards creating sustainable value.

Business leaders continue to be taught to focus on creating shareholder value and delivering the next quarter's results. Therefore, the need for strategic sustainability leadership and investment is absent. The short-term-oriented reward system has contributed significantly to most business leaders not paying adequate attention to sustainability. They continue to be on a perpetual treadmill of delivering short-term results to create shareholder value at any cost. The Cambridge University Institute of Sustainability Leadership, Columbia University's Earth Institute, Stanford, Yale, and Duke are amongst the early adopters, but few other universities and business schools have taken the first step.

Cambridge Institute of Sustainability Leadership director Polly Courtice said[63]

> Over the past twenty-five years, we have seen at first hand just how challenging it is for business leaders to grapple with complex global challenges and to respond in ways which align profitability and sustainability! Business schools have a critical role to play in developing the far-sighted leaders that companies need. Optional Friday afternoon modules on 'Corporate Social Responsibility' will not cut it.

---

[63] Cambridge University Institute of Sustainability Leadership Newsletter June 2015

Unfortunately, this is the status quo in most business schools. In recent times, more and more business leaders acknowledge the need for sustainability, mostly to meet the approval of organisations like the United Nations and activist groups, rather than through conviction! Business has focused on **'doing good to look good'**.

Business leaders need to be inspired to mainstream sustainability into corporate strategies as a means to 'doing good and doing well' at the same time. The global reward system needs to exit its short-term obsession and recalibrate its focus on *strategic corporate sustainability and strategic national sustainability*, which will contribute to global sustainability. The recommended approach is covered in chapter 3, 'The Challenge'.

The Challenge
Strategic Corporate Sustainability

The previous chapters highlight that neither world leaders nor business leaders have prioritised, engaged, or impacted sustainability in the manner required to reverse the irreversible trajectory of climate change and the related sustainability challenges. In order to bring about a step change, the following key steps are essential prerequisites to change the status quo: leaders with triple-bottom-line mindsets, strategic corporate sustainability, and strategic national sustainability.

3.1 Leaders with Triple-Bottom-Line Mindsets

Figure 2 – Sustainability and the Triple
Bottom Line © Ravi Fernando 2012

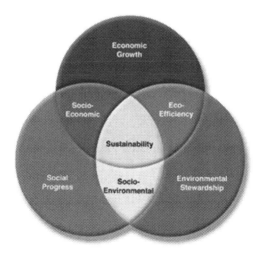

The first and most crucial requirement for a tipping point for sustainability is leaders with 'triple-bottom-line' mindset. For business and national leaders to embed sustainability in strategy, they first need to appreciate the interconnectedness of the triple bottom line of economic, environmental, and social sustainability. The sustainability mindset leader takes every decision through the prism of the triple bottom line. One cannot develop a strategy to impact social, economic, or environmental issues in isolation without taking into consideration socio-economic, socio-environmental, and eco-efficiency impacts. These challenges can no longer be addressed by governments in transition. If business waits for government to take the lead, chances are the reality of climate change and sustainability challenges would have impacted the very survival of the planet and business.

An urgent public-private partnership is required to address all the above issues. In the pre-sustainability era, most businesses and nations took decisions from a one-dimensional economic growth/profitability-at-any-cost perspective. This has led to catastrophic sustainability and climate-change impacts. The short-term shareholder value/GDP growth mindset has to give way to stakeholder and sustainable value creation. The key sustainability challenges need optimal triple-bottom-line solutions, taking into consideration the need for *balancing the social and environmental impacts of every economic growth decision.*

3.2 What Is 'Ideally' Required for a Tipping Point for Sustainability?

For sustainability to impact the planet, we *ideally* need enlightened governments mobilising strategic national sustainability policies and strategies, which in turn will encourage businesses to move to strategic corporate sustainability.

However, a reality check confirms this is unlikely to happen in the short to medium term. It's twenty-two years since the first Earth Summit in Rio, and global carbon emissions and concentrations have increased significantly, as given below. In 2015, the majority of governments subsidise both fossil fuels and deforestation to the tune of US$7-8 trillion per annum.

If one were to look at the past twenty-two years, both global carbon emissions and carbon concentrations in the air have risen dramatically.

Between 1992 to 2014;
- **Global carbon emissions increased from 21 Gt to 32 Gt +52 percent**
- **Global 'air pollution' moved up from** 250ppm to 400ppm **+60 percent**

Most national leaders are focused on GDP/economic growth at any cost, with few exceptions to the rule. Their focus is on winning the next election.

This leads to taking populist actions, irrespective of the impact on the environment. Economic growth (GDP) becomes the overriding influencer of all decisions, despite knowing all the downsides and negative impacts of climate change. Meeting short-term energy needs with coal take priority. The supposedly enlightened nations, the United States, China, the EU, India, and Japan all subsidise fossil fuels; Australia and Canada export coal;

Germany recently invested in coal power; the UK is about to open a fracking site; and Alaska is about to be drilled for oil. The past twenty-two to thirty years confirm the failure of national leaders to address climate change and halt our fossil-fuel-driven obsession. This makes it imperative for *business to lead the way,* considering the rising sphere of influence business has on the global economy and resource utilisation. While the 'idealistic' process outlined in figure 3, 'Requirements for Sustainability', should have been the way forwards, reality demands that sustainable business should lead the way.

Figure 3. Requirements for Sustainability (©RAF2010 November)

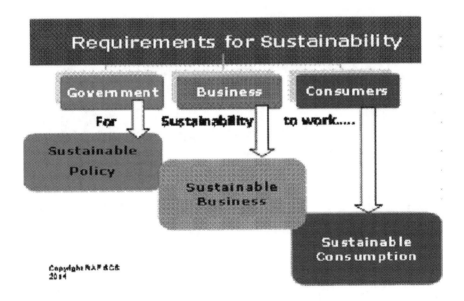

3.3 Sustainable Business Must Lead the Charge

In order to do so, we need enlightened business leaders to embed sustainability in corporate strategy. Business can fashion and influence both government policy and end-user consumption, if it is convinced of the need for sustainability. Therefore, the recommended way forwards is for business to embrace strategic corporate sustainability and influence both strategic national sustainability and sustainable consumption. A few enlightened business leaders have already taken bold steps without any impetus from governments to drive towards sustainable business. However, for global impact, we need *scale*. Unlike at any time in history, the rising influence of business – which is set to occupy over 80 per cent of the top one hundred global economic entity positions in the next decade – demands we harness their potential for good. Most nations depend on business to spearhead their global economic growth: the United States (Wal-Mart, Apple, Microsoft, GE, and Google); Japan (Toyota, Nissan, and Mitsubishi); Germany (Mercedes, BMW, and Henkel); UK (BP, Glaxo Smithkline); South Korea (Samsung, LG). Therefore, if businesses are already on the right track, nations will grow sustainably. The challenge going forward is for nations and businesses to commit to sustainable development and sustainable growth. How a business needs to pursue strategic corporate sustainability is outlined below, and the seven imperatives for doing so are in chapter 4.

3.4 Strategic Corporate Sustainability [64]

"A commitment to implementing strategies for sustainable business which **differentiates the organisation**, whilst impacting all stakeholders which are in its sphere of influence." © Ravi Fernando January 2010

Strategic corporate sustainability is a concept I presented at Cambridge that requires businesses to commit to making strategic

---

[64] Fernando .R(2012), Sustainable globalization, Journal of Corporate Governance Vol.12 No.4 2012 pp.586

decisions for the sustainability of the organisation and the planet. Every business needs to be committed to sustainable business. Business needs to move away from bolt on CSR initiatives (doing good to look good) to strategic corporate sustainability. Today, a host of sustainability challenges pose a significant risk to business, such as climate change, access to strategic resources, major supply-chain disruptions, volatile energy costs, new and complex consumer and customer needs, and changing employee expectations. A host of dynamic start-ups focused on meeting consumer needs more sustainably is already disrupting the best-laid strategic plans of established businesses. Therefore, embedding sustainability is increasingly emerging as an essential **risk-mitigation strategy.** The emerging sustainability challenges threaten the strategic continuity of many of the established business models. The established market leaders, hampered with unsustainable cost infrastructure, will have to compete with new and more agile sustainable business models to survive.

In the past, businesses engaged with sustainability issues from a distance.

The reason is that environmental and social issues were perceived as being the domain and responsibility of national governments. Today, business knows that leaving it solely to national governments, which neither have the resources nor influence to address it, will be a recipe for disaster in most countries. The crisis we face today has been compounded by unsustainable national and business decisions taken in the past thirty years: the dramatic rise in fossil fuel use, deforestation for agriculture, and pollution of groundwater. Therefore, business needs to influence its destiny and strategic survival by embracing sustainability challenges with creative, sustainable solutions.

Sustainability-led decision-making requires a strategic lens and not the prevailing shareholder value, creating short-termism. Most business has engaged with sustainability from a distance, as a 'bolt-on' component to its strategy. Corporate responsibility for most business was confined to CSR (social) initiatives. However, the sphere of influence of business extends to both the environment and society.

Business continues to exploit natural resources; this in turn results in negative impacts on society. Thereafter, businesses most often leave governments to clean up and bear the cost.

Strategic corporate sustainability challenges business to make sustainability its central and pivotal guiding principle as it strives to generate sustainable economic value while being committed to environmental stewardship and societal progress transparently. Global business networks such as the UN Global Compact, World Business Council for Sustainable Development, and the B Corporation initiatives strive to set sustainability standards that guide and direct business to engage with the planet in a more strategic and sustainable way.

Business needs to follow a two-step approach to achieving strategic corporate sustainability as indicated.

Strategic Corporate Sustainability © Ravi Fernando January 2010

3.4.1 *Step 1 - Embed Sustainability in Corporate Strategy*

If a business is to pursue strategic corporate sustainability, its leadership needs to make a commitment to mainstream sustainability as the central focus of its corporate strategy, thereafter creating *one strategy* that will guide and direct the business.

The business needs to follow a two-step process:

Step 1 - Embed sustainability in every element of the strategy, and 'sustainability-proof' it.

The strategy must be augmented with an environmental strategy that helps the business achieve carbon neutrality.

Step 2 - Differentiate the product, service, or offering on a sustainability paradigm, and invest in strategic innovation to create sustainable value.

A commitment to strategic corporate sustainability is a strategic decision that moves away from 'bolt-on' CSR and sustainability.

Embedding Sustainability

Business needs to place sustainability at the epicentre of the business model. Environmental, social, economic, and governance issues should be integrated into corporate strategy. They need to first 'sustainability-proof' the current corporate strategy and thereafter embed sustainability into it.

a) Review and sustainability-proof existing corporate strategy.

Every business has a corporate strategy document that guides its strategy, future investments, and innovation. Most often, this strategy is focused on delivering shareholder value from an economic perspective. The first step is to review the current strategy through the prism of triple-bottom-line thinking and rework it from a sustainability perspective. This will require businesses to take bold actions and rethink many initiatives and investments. This exercise will lead to a sustainability-proofed corporate strategy. In chapter 4.4, 'One Strategy', this step is comprehensively explained.

b) Embed Environmental Sustainability

This step will address future sustainability risks and sustainable business performance indicators (SBPI) by taking into account the materiality of all external environmental risks and challenges to achieve the corporate strategy. This will cover goals to minimise and eventually achieve carbon neutrality by setting aggressive targets to reduce its ecological, water, and carbon footprint. The urgent need for renewable energy and the vulnerability of supply chains will need to be addressed to mitigate the impending risks. Resource utilisation and regeneration needs to be done from a sustainability perspective. In chapter 4.4, 'One Strategy', this is further expanded.

A business/industry-specific *environmental strategy* must form an integral part of its corporate strategy to help it achieve carbon neutrality.

3.4.2 Step 2 - Sustainability-Led Differentiation and Innovation

At step two, an 'enlightened' business moves to create blue oceans of green market spaces by differentiating its offerings on a sustainability paradigm and aligning innovation to sustain it. The business opportunity is to move towards creating new sustainable products and services that meet humanity's needs to substitute the many unsustainable options available today. Creating sustainability-led differentiators will unlock many new green market spaces.

Many leading MNCs have adopted the sustainability-led differentiator approach, e.g., Unilever Sustainable Living Plan, GE Ecomagination, Toyota hybrid cars, and Tesla's electric cars have helped these organisations create new green market spaces. When business takes the lead on sustainability, it will influence sustainable consumption.

3.5 Sustainable Government Policy

Once we have a new cadre of business leaders with triple-bottom-line mindsets, it will influence the national agenda. Though national leaders should have been taking bold steps for sustainable development, they have not had the knowledge, resolve, or impetus to do so. The lobby from businesses committed to 'business as usual' did not help. When business takes the lead for sustainability, governments are better placed to implement policies to ensure the UN sustainable-development goals (September 2015) are focused on and delivered.

Once again, we need to have in place a national leader who champions the cause. Most government policies and strategies in past decades have been focused on achieving economic GDP/GNP growth while decimating natural capital in the guise of achieving national development. An example of such unsustainable policies is the government policy to subsidise the consumption of fossil fuels and deforestation to the tune of US$6.4 trillion per annum, which directly contributes to global warming. Government policy to subsidise deforestation for timber, soya, beef, palm oil, paper and pulp, etc. has contributed to the rapid decimation of more than 50 per cent of global forest cover in the past thirty years. These unsustainable policies and strategies have not taken a triple-bottom-line perspective. They are primarily to drive economic growth at any cost. Decisions like this need enlightened sustainability mindset leaders at the helm to change them. Nations need to review their strategic plans and sustainability-proof each of them, challenging every initiative and plan through the lens of the triple bottom line, and thereafter embed key initiatives for the nation's sustainable utilisation of all resources within its sphere of influence. In order to do so systematically, it should consider adopting strategic national sustainability.

3.6 Strategic National Sustainability [65]

A nation needs to manage the utilisation of its natural resources in a manner whereby both the needs of its present and future generations are not compromised. This can happen only if the nation has sustainable resource-utilisation policies in place for the stewardship of its resources.

Strategic national sustainability is a commitment to implementing sustainable national strategies which differentiates

---

[65] Singapore – A City in a Garden, A Vision for environmental sustainability (INSEAD Case study 2013) pp. 12

the nation, whilst impacting all stakeholders which are in its sphere of influence.

Each nation has the opportunity to sustainably differentiate itself and make its contribution to the new sustainable green economy. The new United Nations Sustainable Development Goals 2015-2030, which replaced the Millennium Development Goals 1990-2014, could form the basis for nations to do so. Strategic national sustainability is no longer an option but a prerequisite for any nation that intends to commit to achieving the new UN Sustainable Development Goals 2015-2030.

A good starting point will be to educate and engage nations' leaders on the subject of sustainable development; ensuring the nation's fossil-fuel dependence is significantly reduced with an accelerated programme to embrace renewable energy will be the game-changer. A sustainability-driven national strategy has triple-bottom-line thinking influencing all decisions. In Singapore, the prime minister leads the national sustainability strategy through the Inter-Ministerial Committee on Sustainable Development, set up in April 2008.[66] The CEO of the nation needs to lead its national sustainability strategy.

Strategic National Sustainability Policy and Strategy

For a tipping point for sustainability to be achieved, we need enlightened leaders to lead the way with a vision for national sustainability. Governments need to develop and implement a strategic national sustainability policy and strategy as the first

---

[66] Singapore – A City in a Garden (INSEAD 2012)

key step to journey towards sustainable development. The key ministries responsible for the economic growth, social progress, and environmental stewardship of the nation need to be unified and empowered under one national sustainability strategy, to secure the strategic interests of the nation from a sustainability perspective. All other ministries could be clustered under one of the three bottom lines, based on their influence and impact. National sustainability strategies need to incentivise all sectors and businesses to pursue the sustainable circular economy. Today, fewer than forty nations have a national sustainability policy, and even fewer have focused sustainability leadership and sustainable resource utilisation. There are ten major focuses that should guide strategic national sustainability policy and strategy:

1) *Reducing Poverty/Inequality of Wealth Distribution*

A social sustainability challenge confirmed by the emergence of the 99 per cent versus 1 per cent global movement. Today, whilst the top 1 per cent control over 46 per cent of global wealth, they are projected to increase it to 52 per cent by 2030. The eighty-five richest individuals have more wealth than the bottom half the world's population. This inequality, if not addressed, will lead to global social instability. Today, the young unemployed and the poor are being coaxed into violent terrorism in many parts of the world, as they are the most unengaged and vulnerable.

2) *Mitigation of Global Warming by Exiting Fossil Fuels*

The urgent need is to exit fossil fuels and increase renewable energy. Fossil fuels account for 68 per cent of electricity generation and transportation. Global carbon emissions moved from 30.2 gigatons in 2010 to 32 gigatons in 2014, and concentrations in the atmosphere reached 400 ppm. The projection is that they would reach 43.2 gigatons by 2019. Global warming is now on an irreversible trajectory to reach a temperature rise of +2°C to 4° C in the medium term; 2014 was already designated the hottest year on record, with temperatures reaching 58.24 F versus 56.75 F and recording a sea-level rise of 56.35 mm. The impending devastating impacts of climate change can only be thwarted if the acceleration towards renewable energy becomes the global priority.

The rise of 'middle-class Asia, Latin America, and Africa' aspiring to a Western lifestyle will contribute to a greater need for energy and accelerated emissions unless a shift to renewable energy has pre-empted it. Many world leaders go about their tasks as though we already have two planets. One is called the water-rich Northern Hemisphere; the other is the Southern Hemisphere, which will face the major brunt of climate-change impact. Exiting fossil fuels, starting with coal, needs to happen in the next ten to fifteen years. An interim measure could be natural gas, whilst making aggressive investments in scaling up solar, wind, wave, and all-new technologies in this space. The 'No Roof Left Behind' campaign in China should be launched in every nation to scale up solar energy dramatically.

3) *Agree about Global Carbon Pricing and Implement it With Urgency*

Unless there is a high cost that deters the use of carbon-emitting fossil fuels, the current 'business as usual' paradigm will continue. Carbon pricing will also make it advantageous for enlightened businesses to take strategic decisions, which immediately gives them a level playing field to compete with low-cost, unsustainable business.

4) *Halt Deforestation and Reforest with Urgency*

As mentioned earlier, halting deforestation has to be an urgent national priority. The decimation of 50 per cent of global forest cover in the past thirty years should be the wake-up call to do so. A good start is to halt all subsidies for deforestation and approvals to do so. The investment required for reforestation has to be the priority and should now be a key element in every national strategy. This will regenerate diminishing forest cover and enable the rain cycle once again. The most significant benefit is that it will increase the forest cover, contributing to absorption of carbon emissions and contributing to a healthier society. The felling of any tree should ideally be a punishable offence, unless a regeneration strategy has first been put in place, where at the time of doing so, another tree is ready to take its place.

5) *Drive Sustainable Consumption*

Nations could structure taxation in such a manner to favour all sustainable purchase decisions, from renewable energy to hybrid/ electric vehicles.

It could encourage purchase of sustainable agriculture. Many strategic initiatives can encourage sustainable consumption if the government is committed to doing so.

6) *Conserve, Protect, and Harvest All Sources of Fresh Water*

Punitive measures should be initiated to prevent businesses from treating the planet like an open sewer. Protecting the nations' freshwater resources should take priority. Rainwater harvesting should be a priority in those nations that have rainfall, and rainwater storage should be enabled in every home.

7) *Eliminate Food Waste and Accelerate Sustainable Agriculture*

The colossal waste of between 30 and 40 per cent of all agricultural produce and processed food is unsustainable. The extraction of these resources and the totally irresponsible manner in which it is summarily deposited in landfills needs to be halted.

8) *Build Low-Carbon Smart Cities*

As 70 per cent of the global population will migrate to urban cities by 2050, creating sustainable infrastructure should be a priority e.g., Policies for public transport. Green spaces must be retained. High technology enabled sharing economies need to be encouraged through policy.

9) *Reduce Global Debt and Global Credit for Unsustainable Consumption*

Most nations have between 40 and 50 per cent of household income tied up in household credit, which simply encourages unsustainable consumption. The current paradigm of 'we can consume as long we can get the credit to do so' is one of the contributory factors to waste and purchase of wants as opposed to needs.

The same malady impacts business and national investment: if we can get credit or borrow, let's do it. In 2015, the current paradigm has piled up global debt to US$ 205 trillion, over twice the current global GDP.

10) *Mobilise National Sustainability Policies to Give an Impetus for Sustainable Business to Flourish*

Encouraging and supporting businesses to pursue strategic corporate sustainability has to be a priority area of focus in national sustainability policy and strategy. It could encourage moving to renewable energy, investing in green buildings and supply chains. Many creative incentives could support sustainable business to flourish over business that persists in unsustainable practices.

Scarcity of material resources is best addressed by the optimal use of existing natural resources, especially with nanotechnology, where 'less is more' presents many opportunities for economic growth sustainably.

The Global Compact Accenture Study in September 2013 mentioned that 83 per cent of CEOs believe that *government sustainability, policy-making, and regulation will be critical to progress.* Public/private partnerships are crucial to achieve this end. New Zealand and Costa Rica have begun the journey. President Obama enacted five executive orders from 2009 to 2015 for sustainability, and China has announced its commitments to exit fossil fuels and invest in renewable energy, whilst the EU has been a trailblazer.

The 2015 UN sustainable-development goals could be the tipping point for all nations to develop a strategic national sustainability policy and strategy blueprint and implement them.

3.7 Sustainable Consumption

For too long, both national policy-makers and businesses have been living in the false hope that end consumers will drive sustainable consumption and that as a result, business will have no option but to fall in line. But the reality is that economies of scale for unsustainable products created a red ocean of low-priced products, along with an insignificant niche for sustainable products at a premium price point. This reality was substantially helped by government subsidies and policies that gave an unfair advantage to unsustainable products and service production. This is the reason it has taken so long for renewable-energy options like solar, wave, and wind power to take off and why forest cover is decimated is the government subsidies for fossil fuels/deforestation. In 2015, the combined government subsidies for fossil fuel and deforestation could be in the region of US$6-7 trillion. The short-sighted policy of China, the United States, Russia, India, Japan, and the EU, which are the top five in terms of fossil-fuel subsidies as per the IMF, has not only sustained climate-change-causing fossil fuels but directly blocked the advent of renewable sources. This is another reason why business will need to change the game as short-sighted government policies influenced by big oil companies (e.g., Exxon, Shell, Caltex, Koch Brothers, et al.) have contributed to the crisis we face. Sustainable business has never had a level playing field to influence the sustainability agenda and has been hamstrung by these short-sighted polices.

However, a few enlightened business leaders have swum against the tide and are winning the battle today, such as Unilever, GE, and Tesla. If strategic corporate sustainability drives governments towards strategic national sustainability policies and strategies, we then have a glimmer of hope for global sustainability. The outcome will be sustainable infrastructure, products, and services for consumers. This will engender 'sustainable consumption' as the scale of sustainable products will increase significantly from niche to mass-market offerings. One of the prerequisites for this to happen is that the end consumer is also enlightened and educated of the urgent need to exercise personal responsibility to make sustainable choices every time. In all three phases, the common factor is that *leaders must be educated and made aware of the urgent need for sustainability.*

For too long, we have assumed that all leaders understood and embraced the need for sustainability. This was a wrong assumption. A majority of business leaders and the former prime ministers of Canada and Australia are a case in point. Most leaders unfortunately do not have a science background and therefore lack the sensitivity to the impending ecological disaster. As outlined below, strategic corporate sustainability and strategic national sustainability need to impact their sphere of influence with policies and strategies that set the platform for a sustainable global economy.

Figure 5-Focus and Sphere of Influence
© Ravi Fernando April 2012[67]

Strategic Corporate Sustainability	Strategic National Sustainability -Focus and Sphere of Influence	Strategic Corporate Sustainability -Focus and Sphere of Influence
Economic Sustainability	Policy/Governance/ Research and Development/Alliances Differentiation/ GDP/GNP	Strategy/Innovation/ R&D/ Differentiation/ Governance Collaboration/Profit/ Cash
Social Sustainability	Policy/Society/ Community/ Health/ Education and Skills	Strategy/Society Employee/Community
Environmental Sustainability	Policy/GHG Emissions/ Renewable Energy Water/Waste/ Green Cover/ Reforestation	Strategy/Carbon Footprint Water/Green Energy/Green Business and Sustainable Innovation/Life Cycle Analysis

- **Business** needs to commit to strategic corporate sustainability. This process should be championed by the CEO and influence national policy on sustainability.

- **Nations** need to embed sustainability in national policy and strategy. They need to set up national sustainability

---

67   Fernando. R(2012), Sustainable Globalization, Journal of Corporate governance Vol.12 no 4 2012 pp.588

steering committees that have key ministries which cover economic, social, and environmental issues.

- **Consumers** the world over need to be enlightened on the need for sustainable consumption by making sustainable choices and being empowered to do so. If businesses and nations are committed to the cause of global sustainability, then sustainable consumption is inevitable.

CHAPTER 4

The Opportunity
Strategic Corporate Sustainability
Seven Imperatives for
Sustainable Business

I conducted an exploratory study in 2013-14 of a UN Global Compact local network in Asia, to understand what conditions business mobilised to embed sustainability in corporate strategy. The selected network had won the Asia Pacific Award and was ranked among the 2014 top ten UNGC local networks. It had more than forty signatory companies, which influenced more than five hundred affiliates and subsidiary organisations. This study was an integral part of my Cambridge studies, which laid the foundation for understanding the key imperatives. The Seven Key Strategic Imperatives emerged from this study and were mobilised by companies that had embedded sustainability in corporate strategy. This was further validated by current literature and best practices of the leading sustainable corporations of the world. The highlights of the study were outlined in chapter 2.1.

4.1) First Imperative

It's Got to Be a Sustainability Mindset CEO

If any business wants to embed sustainability in corporate strategy, sustainability leadership at the top is the essential game-changer. If the CEO had a triple-bottom-line mindset with an appreciation of global sustainability challenges, invariably he or she would translate it to a vision for creating sustainable value. The key characteristic of organisations that made strides towards sustainability was they had a CEO who understood the need to align the business to the new global sustainability agenda.

The common factor amongst the high-sustainability corporations was that the CEO/chairman led embedding sustainability in corporate strategy.

The sustainability leadership impact of CEOs like Paul Polman (Unilever), Jochen Zeitz (Puma), Elon Musk (Tesla), Jeff Immelt (GE), Ray Anderson (Interface), and Anita Roddick (The Body Shop) has transformed organisations. Each of them demonstrated that it's possible to do good and do well at the same time. Their results confirm that triple-bottom-line focus delivers excellent results in the medium to long term.

Paul Polman, the chief executive officer of consumer-goods giant Unilever says, "I don't think our fiduciary duty is to put shareholders first. I say the opposite. What we firmly believe is that if we focus our company on improving the lives of the world's citizens and come up with genuine sustainable solutions, we are more in sync with consumers, society, and ultimately this will result in good shareholder returns.[68]"

Elon Musk, CEO of Tesla, is leading change with a groundbreaking approach to sustainable automobiles. He has beaten all the established giants of the industry – e.g., Toyota, BMW, Ford, GM – to create a new blue-ocean market space for electric vehicles. Tesla electric vehicles have continued to win accolades for efficiency and design. His leadership and strategic investment are ensuring the

---

[68] Paul Polman Unilever 2014

infrastructure is in place. A US Electric charging station network, and investment in three new giga-plants for producing the battery in collaboration with Panasonic will come on stream from 2016. Musk has exploited the irreversible trajectory of the need to exit fossil fuels in the future and set the pace for creating the new electric vehicles green market space.

The UN-sponsored Principles for Responsible Investment Survey in 2014[69] states that **only 8 per cent** of the institutional investor community saw CEOs as effective communicators of ESG-related[70] issues. This means 92 per cent of institutional investors feel that the majority of today's CEOs are unable to communicate the global sustainability agenda either effectively or persuasively. The ability to articulate the need for sustainability can only come with both knowledge and conviction.

Most CEOs have not engaged with the subject to be inspired by it. The UN Global Compact Guide to Corporate Sustainability had this to say:

> Full buy-in from the Chief Executive and the Board of Directors is essential to orient a company towards sustainability for the long term, also by choosing a path of sustainability, leaders are taking responsibility for our shared future-making sure that business plays a key role in solving our world's biggest challenges.

---

[69] Principles of Responsible Investment survey (2014)
[70] ESG - Environmental, social and governance

Being a sustainability mindset leader in a world that has a system geared to reward 'unsustainable performance' based on the short term is a major challenge. Today, CEOs know a quarter's poor performance could jeopardise their future. The pressure to deliver quarterly results robs most CEOs of the time to think strategically and sustainably.

The media accused Paul Polman, Unilever's chief executive, stating that his commitment to sustainability is affecting his ability to deliver aggressive growth. The *Financial Times* of 10 February 2015 had this to say: 'Paul Polman's socially responsible Unilever falls short on growth'.

All triple-bottom-line initiatives have been grouped together as 'CSR/socially responsible initiatives'. However, Polman has been vindicated with the 2015 year-to-date results, which show robust growth with the sustainable brand portfolio outperforming the rest.

Enlightened CEOs will need to be tenacious and not wilt under pressure of the ignorant majority. They need to do so by building a strong board and key stakeholder support for pursuing strategic corporate sustainability. The majority of corporate leaders have not been exposed to the concept of triple bottom line or sustainability at business school. They have risen to key positions delivering short-term results and shareholder value.

John Elkington, in his book, *The Breakthrough Challenge*,[71] refers to four overarching challenges for sustainability: future

---

[71] Elkinton .J and Zeitz. J - The Breakthrough Challenge (2014), Wiley

bottom line, future of incentives, future of investment, and future of leadership. The tipping point will come when the future of leadership is in place. Elkington goes on to elucidate: 'Because the current mind set of competing and consuming primarily for financial gain is unsustainable, business leaders must work together to build the new foundations for tomorrow's growth. Focusing on the need to redefine what it means to be a good leader in business.'

The prerequisite to mobilise sustainability in any organisation is for the number-one person in the organisation, e.g., CEO/chairman/ managing director, to have a sustainability mindset.

4.1.1 Winning Today's Leaders

Any business leader who is convinced and willing to change towards being a triple-bottom-line mindset leader needs to be supported on the journey to create a sustainable business. The fact remains that the majority of today's business leaders have unfortunately not been exposed to the concept of triple bottom line or sustainability. The challenge is to win them over by presenting the opportunity for growth. This has to be done in a sensitive manner that does not alienate, distance, or threaten them in any way. They have risen to these key positions by performing and delivering short-term results and shareholder value. They need to unlearn this paradigm and move to be leaders who deliver strategic, sustainable results for the business by creating sustainable value for all stakeholders.

4.1.2 Building Tomorrow's Leaders

Business schools, academia, peers (e.g., Plan B corporation) have a major role to get the incumbent and future leaders evangelised for sustainability with urgency. Developing future business leaders with a sustainability mindset should be the urgent priority of all business schools. Sustainability strategy needs to be a mandatory course in all MBA curricula. It's been more than twenty years since Rio 1992,[72] and a handful of business schools have it in the curriculum. Every year that passes, we create another cohort of single-bottom-line-focused, short-term-oriented 'shareholder-value-creating' leaders who will not know how to build sustainable value.

Business schools should urgently mainstream strategic corporate sustainability as a mandatory subject whilst building in sustainability modules to the current core subjects of finance, operations, strategy, marketing, innovation, and talent management. It's the dean's job to make this happen and ensure all business school curricula are relevant for today's global agenda. The reality confirms the urgency with which we need to instil the subject in the hearts and minds of every single leader. Business schools and all universities need to have a sense of urgency and resolve the 'internal politics' that have prevented the changes required so far and mainstream sustainability in all business curriculums. Warren Bennis said, 'Leadership is the ability to translate vision into reality.' The need of the hour is for all leaders to be first educated on the subject to be able to create a vision for sustainable business.

---

[72] UN Earth Summit Climate Conference Rio (1992)

Leadership Is the Key

There were three types of business leaders identified earlier in chapter 2, and their disposition to sustainability can be summed up as follows:

- Unprepared leaders – unaware and deny sustainability
- Reactive/anticipatory leaders – compliance-driven, CSR-focused
- Integrated/aligned leaders – committed to 'one strategy'

The majority of today's business leaders seem to fall into the first two categories, and as mentioned earlier, would account for between 90 and 97 per cent of all business leaders if one were to consider both listed and unlisted organisations. A very small group of leaders, between 2 and 3 per cent, are sustainability mindset leaders who champion, frame, and position the cause.

What Will Not Help?

- the second in command, e.g., a chief operating officer/vice president/deputy chairman wanting sustainability to be mobilised in the organisation and not the CEO, chairman, or president
- a number one who believes in sustainability but does not have the leadership to align the rest of the top team
- business schools including an elective like ethics or corporate social responsibility in the curriculum

What Is Needed?

- a leader who understands the need for a sustainable planet
- a leader who knows there is no future in unsustainable business
- a leader who sees the growth opportunity for sustainable business and creates new green market spaces for sustainable products and services
- a leader who aligns the board and the organisation to follow his vision
- a leader who inspires all stakeholders towards a vision for sustainability
- business schools that are committed to creating future leaders with triple-bottom-line mindsets
- shareholders who invest in sustainable business for the long term

---

Strategic Corporate Sustainability – The Triple Bottom Line

It's got to be a sustainability mindset CEO.

The responsibility for hiring a sustainability mindset leader as CEO is with the board. All boards that want their business to be relevant in the long term urgently need to establish if the current CEO has the credentials. Boards must ensure they have the right leader for the future sustainability of the business and dismiss the current CEO if he or she is not willing to embrace sustainability with urgency. The wrong CEO will deliver short-term results but sacrifice its long-term sustainability and survival. *The bottom line is that every business and nation needs a triple-bottom-line mindset leader today.*

4.2) *Second Imperative*

Framing and Positioning Sustainability

The sustainability mindset CEO must frame and position sustainability as the core guiding principle of the strategy and in addition, present sustainability as an opportunity to drive future growth. They need to win the support and commitment of the board and all stakeholders to the vision for sustainable value creation.

Creating a sustainability culture in the organisation is important, as Benn, Dunphy, and Griffiths (2007)[73] elucidate. The visionary framing of sustainability as an opportunity to create blue oceans of green market spaces and driver of sustainable innovation will inspire all cadres. As business embeds sustainability, it will generally evolve from a stage of compliance to efficiency and finally to differentiation/innovation as it matures.

In every stage, the way sustainability is framed and positioned by the CEO/board will determine how the organisation engages with sustainability.

Apple CEO Tim Cook had this to say after his bold and strategic investment in a 280-megawatt first solar farm in Monterey County: 'Quite frankly, we're doing this because it's the right thing to do, but you may also be interested to know that it's good financially to do it.'[74] Apple, with the world's largest market capitalisation

---

[73]   Benn, S Dunphy .D and Griffiths. A (2007), Enabling change for Corporate sustainability: An Integrated Perspective, Australian Journal of Environmental management – Volume 13 pp.156-157

[74]   http://www.greenbiz.com/article – Apple, Google and the evolving economics of energy-Greenbiz 13 Feb 2015

of US$741.8 billion as of May 2015, is strategically using its cash reserves to secure sustainable energy. Google has done the same with NextEra Energy resources for wind energy. Both organisations are framing and positioning their commitment to sustainable business amongst all their stakeholders.

Paul Polman, the Unilever CEO, did the same when he launched the 'Unilever Sustainable Living Plan' internally to the 140,000-plus employees and thereafter positioned the strategy to all its stakeholders. Polman leads the way as a role model for all present and future CEOs who intend on creating sustainable value.

The CEO/board must lead the internalisation of sustainability across the organisation and sanction the investments needed to do so. The management/leadership team must drive its execution and progress. The operations team must be energised to drive sustainability in the front line. The organisation needs to create a sustainability culture to retain its focus.

Time invested to internalise sustainability is time well spent, as everyone in the organisation needs to be convinced of the new vision and purpose that drives the organisation. It makes sense for any organisation wanting to pursue the journey to garner the support of global sustainability champions and seek their advice on how they positioned sustainability in their organisation.

The Board
Unless this key influencer group is convinced of the need to embed sustainability in both the vision and strategy of the organisation, there is no way they will support initiatives or

sanction the investment. Therefore, the first responsibility is to 'frame and position' a compelling sustainability vision and strategy at the board level. The board needs to take this vision and communicate it to all stakeholders in a systematic way as the new direction the business will take and its strategic benefits.

The Management/Leadership Team

Once the board approves the one strategy, the management/leadership team will align behind it and drive the strategy through the organisation. The CEO needs to frame and position the sustainability-led 'one strategy' effectively to engage and inspire the top team. It is crucial that the CEO appoints a VP/director/CSO (Chief Sustainability Officer) to mobilise the sustainability agenda to operationalise the strategy.

The Operations Team

The operations team is the front line of the business, and they need to be convinced and energised to implement the strategy in the front line. Many an organisation with sustainability ambitions has failed as their front line was not engaged in the strategy. The CEO must inspire the top team for this to happen and engage with the front-line team to be the cheerleader.

The Organisation

Internalising the new sustainability strategy across the organisation is a key step for any business that wants to engage its cadres to tread the new path. The GSCS 'ideas' approach is an excellent way to do so and is outlined later on in Key Imperative Four, 'One Strategy'.

The way Jan Carlzon, Scandinavian Air Service CEO, launched his concept of 'Moments of Truth' in the 1990s to create a new customer-driven organisation is a good model to follow. The CEO is the one responsible for leading each of the above groups towards the new sustainability vision, as Paul Polman of Unilever has done with great passion and drive. The role of framing and positioning sustainability is equally applicable to national strategy.

What Will Not Help?
- the CEO sending out a memorandum on the importance of sustainability
- notice boards with posters on the new green strategy
- PR and publicity of company initiatives and CSR activity
- having a CSR/sustainability department that has no investment, credibility, or power
- communicating in public and not implementing the strategy

What Is Needed?
- a moment-of-truth zeal to engage all stakeholders
- a level of transparency that wins the hearts and minds of the public
- clarity of purpose, vision, and strategy for creating a sustainable business
- alignment of board, CEO, management, and all employees

What is required is an approach where the CEO takes the lead and creates a Jan Carlzon[75] moment-of-truthlike zeal in touching the hearts and minds of every employee to understand and

---

[75] Carlzon. Jan - Moments of Truth (1987)

implement the new strategy in an empowered and strategic way in every interaction.

It must be emphasised that having done so, implementation must take pride of place. Many an organisation's bold public commitments on sustainability fail due to the lack of tenacity to implement them. All key stakeholders should be apprised of progress versus commitments. Most organisations tend to go quiet till an NGO raises the question. It's also prudent to under-promise when communicating to the public but over-deliver on sustainability commitments. The literature refers to creating a sustainability culture as espoused by Benn, Dunphy, and Griffiths (2007). The organisation could adopt the Global Strategic Corporate Sustainability 'IDEAS'[76] approach where internalisation > differentiation and embedding of strategy > activation and strategic review is followed in that sequence.

We need to position and frame sustainability as one that will:

- deliver sustainable business, albeit strategically, and not in the short term, a key factor all stakeholders need to understand
- inspire and drive its innovation and R&D agenda
- contribute to an engaged and purpose-driven workforce/ supply chain
- be good for business and the planet simultaneously

One of the key responsibilities of the sustainability mindset CEO is to mobilise sustainability across the organisation by presenting a compelling vision and strategy that resonates across

---

[76]   © Global Strategic Corporate Sustainability Pvt. Ltd 'IDEAS'(2015)

the organisation as a timely, believable, achievable, and strategic business strategy that's good for business, the planet, and all its stakeholders.

Strategic Corporate Sustainability – The Triple Bottom Line

Framing and positioning the concept of the triple bottom line and how it has been embedded in the 'one' strategy needs to be communicated in both word and deed. It must be done in a planned, inspiring, and engaging manner. This is an essential prerequisite for any business committed to sustainability.

The emphasis and priority the CEO/board attaches to the organisation's sustainability-led strategy will be sensed by every employee based on how it's framed, positioned, and prioritised. Measurement, regular reviews, and rewards for sustainability-led initiatives will immediately confirm the priority the CEO/board attaches to the strategy.

4.3) Third Imperative

Sustainability Enabling Governance

The board of directors' first responsibility is to see that the organisation has a sustainability-mindset CEO at the helm to ensure the organisation is relevant and sustainable in the future. As mentioned in the earlier chapter, if the board concludes the current CEO does not have the orientation for sustainability, then it needs to take one of two decisions. It must either bring the CEO up to speed with a programme of mentorship and sustainability education which achieves that end in the short term or must hire a new CEO. Thereafter, the board must set the tone and give the organisation's CEO the support needed to pursue the sustainability agenda.

The board's next responsibility is to review its corporate strategy, to ensure it is sustainability-proofed and build in sustainable business performance indicators **(SBPI).** The board has a pivotal role to ensure sustainability governance prevails. It needs to install the structure and process required for the organisation to move in this direction.

One of the key questions the chairman needs to ask is, *does the board have sustainability-mindset leaders who are up to speed with the new global agenda for sustainability?* The reality is that in a majority of companies, they do not have such individuals on boards today.

The role of the chairman of the board will need to be redefined to augment the following key sustainability-governance-enabling actions. He needs to populate the board with sustainability mindset talent which have the right functional expertise, geographical exposure, and gender mix; have the **right** sustainability-mindset CEO in place; and focus the business on mitigating sustainability risks proactively as it strives to achieve its sustainability-driven corporate strategy and commercial goals.

Most business organisations will need to review their board composition and current level of engagement/knowledge of the organisation's future sustainability risks. CEOs and boards will need to replace those who have not embraced the new global agenda at all levels with those who have.

It will be crucial for the CEO to get the board up to speed on the global macro-industry view and identify specific long-term sustainability challenges and opportunities. Similarly, he or she needs to update the board with the key relevant global and regional trends that will impact business and sustainability performance in both the short and medium term.

The key conditions sustainable business mobilised, as Eccles, Ioannou, and Serafeim (2011)[77] identified were that they 'assigned formal responsibility around sustainability to the Board and set up a separate board committee that deals with sustainability issues and linked compensation to sustainable performance.' Eccles, Ioannou, and Serafeim (2012)[78], Lubin and Esty (2010)[79] confirm the above are essential to move the sustainability agenda forward in any organisation.

Board-Level Sustainability Governance

Ensuring the future sustainability and relevance of the organisation is the key role of the board. Therefore, it becomes crucial for the board to be up to speed with the global

---

[77] Eccles .R, Ioannou. I and Serafeim .G, (2011) Harvard Business review Impact of a Corporate Culture of sustainability on Corporate Behaviour and performance, Harvard Business school working paper (12-035) November 25th, 2011 pp.1 2011

[78] Eccles .R, Ioannou. I and Serafeim .G Harvard Business review Impact of a Corporate Culture of sustainability on Corporate Behaviour and performance, Harvard Business school working paper (12-035) November 25th, 2011 pp.1 (2012)

[79] Lubin .D .A and Esty .D .C (2010) The Sustainability Imperative - Lessons from leaders from previous game changing megatrends

sustainability agenda. The UN Global Compact LEAD Board Programme is one resource many organisations can access, provided they are signatories to the compact. Business schools have the opportunity to create similar programmes to augment the new demand.

All key decisions that impact investment and capital expenditure, e.g., sustainable innovation and infrastructure alternatives and setting sustainability-driven key performance measures, need to be led by the CEO and board. The board needs to engage with stakeholders wherever the business operates geographically, to ensure all decisions are taken understanding the ground reality from a strategic sustainability point of view. CEOs and boards must also create an incentive structure to reward excellence in sustainability performance, sustainability initiatives, and sustainable creativity and innovation.

Board Nominations Committee

The review of existing board members and the selection of future board members must be done with great care by the chairman or nominations committee, to ensure every board member meets the following criteria: sustainability mindset, functional expertise, and global and regional exposure. The setting up of a board sustainability committee is recommended to give greater focus. The CEO should derive strength and stability from the sustainability committee, which will oversee sustainability measurement, reporting, and rewards of the organisation's performance and ecological impacts.

What Will Not Help?
- if the board is not up to speed with the global sustainability challenges
- if the board does not see the urgency for a sustainable business model
- in family business, a member who does not understand the sustainability agenda
- if the board is not aligned and agreed on the future risks to the business and supply chain posed by climate change
- hoping for the board to accept and support sustainability initiatives versus short-term shareholder value-creating initiatives if they have not bought into the sustainability agenda
- short-term result generation is prioritised to compromise strategic sustainability-led decision-making

What Is Needed?
- competent and enlightened board members who understand the future risks the planet and business are faced with
- the CEO, CSO, and board being of one accord regarding strategy
- a board that supports the CEO's strategic direction

Unlike at any other time, sustainability challenges and climate change can thwart the best-laid plans of any business and significantly hamper its ability to perform. Today, many global, local, and regional sustainability risks and challenges impact business performance. In some cases, they can be predicted and impacts minimised. The boards of the future will need to focus on creating sustainable value, not short-term shareholder value.

> ## Strategic Corporate Sustainability – The Triple Bottom Line
>
> **For sustainability-enabling corporate governance** to prevail in any organisation, it will require a competent sustainability-mindset chairman, board, and CEO. The chairman will need to re-examine its board composition and CEO from the perspective of commitment to sustainable business and make urgent changes if necessary. If the chairman, board, and CEO are proponents of the old shareholder value paradigm, it needs to reinvent itself to embrace the new stakeholder-focused sustainable-value-creation paradigm. Ensuring the organisation mitigates sustainability challenges and business risks whilst creating new green market spaces to deliver sustainable value for all its stakeholders will be the new mandate for all boards.

4.4) Fourth Imperative

'One' Strategy which Embeds Sustainability in Corporate Strategy

The 2015 Ethical Corporation Survey[80] amongst 472 respondents from around the world asked what the top three sustainability trends were. Responses were as follows:

- 45 per cent stated that embedding sustainability in strategy was the priority.
- 30 per cent stated sustainable innovation is key to the future.
- 25 per cent mentioned that sustainability was a key business driver.

---

[80]   Ethical Corporation (January 2015) Top Sustainability trends for 2015

However, in reality, most organisations have a corporate strategy and a separate CSR/sustainability strategy. What is required today is to create *one strategy* by embedding sustainability in the corporate strategy. Any business that has ambitions to pursue sustainability needs to do so strategically and systematically.

4.4.1 Review Corporate Strategy and Sustainability-Proof It

Over the years, businesses have focused on developing a vision, goals, and corporate strategy/strategic plan that guide their investment, actions, and economic growth. They have served business well and driven unprecedented economic growth, global expansion, and shareholder value. However, most businesses operate in crowded red oceans of aggressive competition. A few create new blue oceans of opportunity like Apple has done in the past decade. The key issue with the current corporate strategy-development process is that little or no attention is paid to the **environmental and social bottom lines**. They are focused on delivering economic profit and shareholder value at any cost. The sustainability-proofed corporate strategy will need to address the following:

- establish the true cost of externalities
- establish and prioritise actions based on materiality
- establish a strategy to access raw material and resources
- eliminate waste
- increase collaboration for sustainable innovation
- ensure stakeholder buy-in
- eliminate negative societal and environmental impacts
- focus on strategic sustainable growth

Sustainability demands a new triple-bottom-line prism to be applied to the current corporate strategy initiatives and challenge every assumption from that perspective. All decisions, actions, and initiatives need to consider the socioeconomic, eco-efficiency and socio–environmental impacts prior to being agreed as a strategy initiative. The past practice of developing two independent strategies, corporate strategy and a bolt-on CSR/CR/sustainability addendum, is history. As mentioned earlier, the existing corporate strategy needs to be sustainability-proofed and risk-mitigation strategies built into it.

4.4.2 Create Strategy to Unlock Blue Oceans of Green Market Spaces

Creating blue oceans of green market spaces is the most compelling business opportunity that should drive all business to embed sustainability in corporate strategy. The need for integrating sustainability into corporate strategy is referred to by Epstein and Roy (2003)[81], Lubin and Esty (2010)[82], and Bonn and Fisher (2011).[83] One strategy features a sustainability vision that guides and propels the organisation, where every function and division in the organisation has clear sustainability-led goals, objectives, and strategies. The following organisations have all created new green market spaces, which they dominate: the

---

[81] Epstein. M and Roy .M .J (2003), Making the case for Sustainability, Linking social and environmental performance actions to financial performance, JCC9 Spring 2003 © Greenleaf publishing, pp.1

[82] Lubin .D .A and Esty .D .C (2010) The Sustainability Imperative – Lessons from leaders from previous game changing megatrends

[83] Bonn .I and Fisher .J (2011), Sustainability: The missing ingredient in strategy, Journal of Business strategy, Vol.32 Iss.1 pp 6

Unilever Sustainable Living Plan[84], GE's Ecomagination[85], M&S Plan A, and Wal-Mart Sustainability 360.[86] Interface, Patagonia, Puma, Tesla, M&S, IKEA, and Novartis are among the leaders in moving in this direction.

Each of them has created a new green market space that did not exist before and commands a premium that addresses the reality of resource constraints with sustainable product and service solutions. This is a growth opportunity for all businesses.

As Daniel Esty says[87]

In a world where natural resource constraints, pressures for greater pollution control is changing market dynamics and climate change impacts promise to be an ever bigger factor in terms of business success, companies will find a growing logic for spelling out their sustainability vision and strategy.

It is crucial that business signals its commitment to sustainability by focusing on strategic results, not quarterly results, as Unilever has done. Too many organisations pay lip service to sustainability by making grandiose narrative commitments but do little to advance the agenda.

---

[84] Unilever Sustainable Living Plan- *www.**unilever**.com/**sustainable-living**-2014*
[85] GE Ecomagination - *www.**ge**.com/about-us/**ecomagination***
[86] Walmart 360 - *corporate.**walmart**.com/microsites/global...report.../**sustainability360**.html*
[87] Esty. Daniel (2014), "How to make Wall street notice sustainability leaders", Green Biz.com 2014-09-02

Many initiatives are launched that are 'green wash' and a cosmetic exercise at best. Drucker[88] referred to this phenomenon as 'doing good to look good', and the end result is 'cosmetic CSR' at best. CSR on its own is far removed from mainstreaming sustainability in corporate strategy. At best, a CSR strategy focuses on the social sustainability aspects and is not an overarching triple-bottom-line approach.

4.4.3 Mandatory Environmental Stewardship

Environmental sustainability is non-negotiable and a key imperative for every business that is focused on creating a sustainability-driven 'one strategy'. In order to do so, it must value and take stock of all natural capital within its sphere of influence from a materiality point of view. Thereafter, business needs to have initiatives to preserve, regenerate, and increase the natural capital stock it inherited or benefits from. The sphere of influence covers all locations globally and all supply chains.

This strategy should measure and initiate actions to move the organisation to carbon neutrality by identifying sustainable business performance indicators (SBPIs), which are relevant and material to the business as given below.

- reducing its global ecological, water, CO_2/GHG footprint
- increasing 'green cover' within its sphere of influence
- moving to renewable energy and taking control of energy needs
- reducing the water footprint and enabling rainwater harvesting

---

[88] Drucker .P and Lee .N, Corporate Social Responsibility (2005) John Wiley & sons Inc.

- managing the life cycle of its products and services
- minimising and eliminating waste and pollution
- engaging in sustainable sourcing and distribution

Irrespective of what industry it operates in, every business needs to strive for carbon neutrality with a sense of urgency. Global stock exchanges and financial institutions need to make it mandatory that every business measures and reports its ecological, water, and carbon footprints, along with the waste and pollution it creates.

Today, Apple, IKEA, Google, Wal-Mart, BMW, and Volkswagen are leading the way with significant investment in solar and wind energy to secure their energy needs from renewable energy. In 2014, at Climate Week in New York, many business leaders agreed to a declaration on renewable energy. It states as follows:

> Accelerating the scale-up of renewable energy will help us deliver a better, healthier more sustainable world for what will soon be 9 billion people. Renewable energy investment is also a smart business opportunity. In addition to providing clean power for a business, renewable energy investment can provide financial returns compatible with and in most cases even higher than other mainstream investment options.[89]

---

[89] State of Green Business: Business leads in renewable power - GreenBiz 19 March 2015

Among the many reasons why businesses will benefit from moving to one strategy is that strategically, sustainability will lower costs; deliver better margins, higher capital value, and ROI; create customer engagement; attract sustainability-mindset millennials; and contribute to health and wellness, which will lead to better business performance and a greener planet.

Finally, the 'one strategy' is made up of:

1) **a sustainability-proofed corporate strategy**
   +
2) **the strategy to create blue oceans of new green market spaces (sustainability-led differentiator and innovation)**
   +
3) **mandatory environmental stewardship/SBPIs to achieve carbon neutrality**

4.4.4 Implementing the One Strategy and GSCS 'IDEAS'

Implementing the one strategy in a manner that engages all employees, impacts the marketplace, and contributes to the sustainability of the business and the planet is the next task ahead. The process created by Global Strategic Corporate Sustainability IDEAS[90] is recommended.

Phase 1 – Internalisation

Inspiring all cadres by engaging them in the new one strategy is crucial to the final implementation. The entire organisation – its top, middle, and frontline employees – need to be educated on

---

[90] **Global Strategic Corporate Sustainability Pvt. Ltd** is a sustainability consulting organization set up in 2015.

the subject of sustainability and the company's commitment to creating sustainable value. Depending on the complexity of the business, cadre, and locations, this could take time but needs to be viewed as an investment. Every business that is committed to moving in this direction must adopt an approach whereby its CEO/HRD team work towards adopting the three 'E' principles of fair process:[91]

a) **Engagement** – Engage with every key employee in a logical and practical manner, covering the top, middle, and frontline employees and its supply chain of its new commitment to a sustainability-driven corporate strategy.

b) **Explanation** – Clearly explain the rationale why sustainability will be the central theme of the company strategy and why this is crucial for both the business and the planet. Frame and position sustainability as a business-growth strategy.

c) **Expectation Clarity** – Before the strategy is rolled out, there must be a concerted effort to ensure it has been clearly understood and that all expectations are clarified. This must be done both internally and externally, with employees, supply-chain partners, shareholders, and others. Periodic updates and reviews, once implementation is off the ground, are crucial to keep all stakeholders engaged.

Phase 2 - Differentiation and Embedding One Strategy

Once the internalisation process is completed, the organisation needs to develop its sustainability-led differentiator, which will unlock blue oceans of green market spaces. As outlined earlier,

---

[91] Chan Kim .W and Mauborgne (2005)- Blue Ocean strategy, Harvard Business school publishing corporation, Page 176-177

the one strategy has three components: sustainability-proofed corporate strategy + creating blue oceans of new green market spaces (sustainability-led differentiator) + mandatory environmental stewardship/SBPIs. Once developed, the next step is to roll out the one strategy, embedding it top-down in all locations using the three-E process, especially amongst the frontline employees. Even the best of companies fail to do so. Many MNCs tend to save the costs associated with rolling out the strategy, and most times, their regional and country teams are in the dark regarding the new strategy. They all have great sustainability strategies on paper at headquarters, but the troops on the field and the supply-chain partners have no clue about it. The best examples of one strategy in the corporate world are

- The Unilever Sustainable Living Plan
- GE's Ecomagination
- M&S Plan A
- Wal-Mart 360

Every one of them followed the internalisation process across the business and energised all cadres to engage with the new vision. Each of them has delivered.

- Unilever is well on the way to double growth but half its environmental impacts.
- General Electric's Ecomagination created US$160 billion in revenue and lowered energy costs by 33 per cent, GHGs by 16 per cent, and water by 47 per cent between 2005 and 2013.

- M&S/Wal-Mart's impact across many supply chains since implementing PLAN A & Wal-Mart 360 have been profound.

Every one of them first delivered some quick wins and lowered costs to win the support of boards and employees. Each of the organisations had significant savings from reducing its environmental impacts.

Phase 3 - Activation

The one strategy, once embedded internally, needs to be taken to the market and activated with all stakeholders. External communication is now a priority in order to ensure all current and potential future customers are aware of the new sustainable products and services. The most effective way to do so is *not* to invest in advertising but to create a coalition for credibility, which takes the message independently to convince end consumers and customers of the sustainability of the offering on all global platforms including social media.

Phase 4 - Strategic Review

Regular and disciplined reviews of the one strategy implementation is recommended to ensure the strategy is dynamic, responsive, and relevant.

What Will Not Help?

- continuing business with multiple strategies and hoping for change
- having two strategies but framing and positioning it as one
- having one strategy but allocating the financial and human resources to achieving economic growth at any cost.

- being ready to change strategy for short-term economic gains
- compromising sustainability-led decisions for shareholder value creation

What Is Needed?

- a seamless alignment of the board, CEO, CSO, and all cadres to the vision for sustainable growth versus business as usual
- alignment and integration of the three components of one strategy
- a belief that this is the right strategy for sustainable growth
- a commitment to strategic corporate sustainability of the business

Strategic Corporate Sustainability - The Triple Bottom Line

One Strategy

The one strategy is made up of:

1) **the sustainability-proofed corporate strategy**
   +

2) **strategy to create blue oceans of green market spaces with sustainability-led differentiation and innovation**
   +

3) **mandatory environmental strategy/SBPIs to achieve carbon neutrality**

Embedding sustainability in corporate strategy to create one strategy is essential to give the entire business one focus to rally round.

The one strategy should articulate a compelling vision where every economic decision has been taken from the perspective of triple-bottom-line impact. Every business needs to have a mandatory environmental stewardship to minimise its ecological, water, and carbon footprints and eliminate waste and pollution.

Engaging and inspiring every employee and supply-chain partner to implement it is as crucial as its development. Adopting the global strategic corporate sustainability IDEAS process is recommended – *internalisation > differentiation and embedding of strategy > activation* and strategic review.

[92]   © Global Strategic Corporate Sustainability Pvt. Ltd 'IDEAS'(2015)

4.5) Fifth Imperative

Sustainability Measurement, Reporting, and Rewards

Any business committed to following the path of sustainability that has mobilised its one strategy needs to measure and report progress in a focused, engaging, and transparent manner. As we know, what gets measured and rewarded is focused on by the team. Once a business commits to the path of sustainability, it needs to have a sustainability team that is responsible for measurement and reporting. As Jan Leschly, the former CEO of Smithkline Beecham, used to tell us, 'If you are not measuring and keeping score, you're just practicing.'

One of the first tasks is to establish the 'as-is' position of what the current *ecological, carbon, and water footprints* are. It needs to measure all internal and external impacts the company has, such as waste to landfill, per cent of energy secured through renewable energy, impact on deforestation, water use, and all externalities. Each organisation needs to identify all factors that are material to business performance and that impact the planet, in order to establish a baseline of its footprint on the planet. In addition, each should analyse the materiality of all activities it engages in within its sphere of influence, e.g., supply chain, to prioritise what elements it needs to focus on and strive to impact from a sustainability perspective to develop the 'to-be' sustainability strategy.

Any organisation not disclosing sustainable business performance indicators should *not* be listed in any stock exchange until such time as they do. For this to happen, we need enlightened stock exchanges that see the power they wield to impact business sustainability.

Today we have a bolt-on approach, where a handful of enlightened businesses get listed in the sustainability indexes, and guess what – over 90 per cent just don't bother. The Global Reporting Initiatives – G4 reporting format and the CERES blueprint are recommended to guide business regarding all the key sustainability impacts it needs to measure and monitor in order to develop a sustainability report.

Independent third-party validation of all sustainability reports will increase its global credibility. The startling fact that emerged from the Corporate Knight's research in 2014 is that only 3 per cent of the world's largest listed companies even report sustainability. If business has ambitions of being sustainable, this figure must reflect that and improve substantially. Independent organisations should measure the organisations' footprint periodically and transparently, where facts and data are presented and evaluated by all stakeholders.

Business needs to proactively recalibrate the strategy regularly based on the sustainability challenges it faces to stay relevant. Each business needs to identify and define a set of sustainable business performance indicators (SBPIs) that reflect materiality and strategic intent. They need to reflect both prevailing and future sustainability challenges. They should be agreed upon and reviewed periodically with the CEO or board as being the right SBPIs to focus on. SBPIs need to be specific to the business and industry it operates in, taking into account global, regional trends and risks. In order to enhance sustainability reporting clear SBPIs, centralised responsibility for measurement and software system to track sustainability results is key (e.g., turnkey systems).

4.5.1 Quarterly to Strategic Reporting

Unilever and Tesla are two organisations that have attracted investment based on their strategic commitment to sustainability as they create blue oceans of green market spaces. When the CEO of Unilever took a stand not to report quarterly performance,[93] it was a clarion call for strategic investment and mind shift from the existing short-term paradigm.

Unilever has abandoned quarterly reporting to discourage executives chasing short-term goals at the expense of realising long-term, sustainable ambitions. While Unilever intends on doubling its business by creating new green market spaces, it hopes to achieve this goal by halving its ecological, carbon, and water footprint whilst significantly reducing its waste and pollution.

Tesla's visionary leader is creating a blue ocean green market space and infrastructure for electric vehicles to bring about a step change where fossil fuels will no longer power them. The 24-million-square-foot new battery manufacturing giga-plants in Nevada are expected to boost production beyond 500,000 Tesla cars[94] with a strategic joint investment from Panasonic and Tesla.

---

[93]   Unilever CEO Paul Polman message to investors in 2014
[94]   treehugger – Transportation, Michael Graham Richard 13 July 2015

4.5.2) Rewarding Sustainability Initiative

Linking compensation and rewards to sustainability performance that contributes to the organisation is the best way to engage employees and attract the right talent. An incentive system that recognises sustainability-led innovation to reward creativity will inspire and challenge multifunctional teams to significantly improve the organisation's sustainable business ideas. Linking compensation to sustainable performance was one of the conditions identified by Eccles, Ioannis, and Serafeim (2011) to contribute to sustainable business.

- **Recruitment and Retention**: Business could incorporate sustainability criteria into recruitment protocols, employee performance appraisals, compensation, and incentives.
- **Training and Development**: Business should consider developing induction programmes on sustainability for all its employees and more advanced programmes on key sustainability issues to sensitise all relevant employees. They could also facilitate coaching, mentoring, and networks for sustainability knowledge sharing.
  Promoting Sustainable Lifestyles: Business needs to define its sphere of influence and use every opportunity to promote sustainable lifestyle choices through innovative benefits, e.g., supporting them to secure renewable energy and reduce waste.

Sustainability measurement, reporting, and review are key steps to ensuring the one strategy is implemented and responsive to the dynamic environment. This is an opportunity to raise the bar for sustainability within the organisation.

What Will Not Help?

- a glossy sustainability report that features CSR activity
- winning CSR and sustainability awards but not having one strategy
- investing funds in PR and publicity
- talking about sustainability but not reporting on sustainability measures
- avoiding reporting poor performance and crises
- doing a sustainability report to get a tick in the box

What Is Needed?

- a commitment to measuring and reporting of all key sustainability measures
- the board reviewing sustainability performance as a priority
- CEO/board creating incentives for sustainability-led innovation
- linking sustainability performance to compensation
- engaging all employees to unleash their potential for creating a sustainable business

---

Strategic Corporate Sustainability – The Triple Bottom Line Sustainability Measurement, Reporting, and Rewards

Business needs to be measuring its ecological, water, and carbon footprints and selected sustainable business performance indicators (SBPIs). Thereafter, report on them transparently. Sustainability-enabling incentives and rewards will engage and inspire the business to deliver excellence at all levels.

4.6) Sixth Imperative

Strategic Stakeholder Engagement

Business needs to move away from the shareholder value-creation mindset and embrace all stakeholders in their sphere of influence. Identifying all stakeholders could be done from a from a triple-bottom-line impact point of view e.g., employees, society, community, supply-chain partners, environment, government, NGOs, and all other public entities that impact its ability to deliver sustainable results. In the past, the reason business gave low priority to stakeholders is because shareholder value creation was always the overriding focus. Chris Laszlo[95] refers to the change needed amongst business leaders:

'The transformation of mindset and organisational culture to include key stakeholders is what enables sustainability to become an essential part of business conduct' (Laszlo 2003).[96]

The new paradigm demands a major departure from the past for CEOs and boards who were measured only on shareholder value creation. They will need to unlearn the past message of 'deliver shareholder value at any cost' to strategic sustainable value creation. It is also in the strategic interest of all organisations to develop partnerships with NGOs, universities, and think tanks, which can add value to business operations.

---

[95] Laszlo. Chris (2003) - The Sustainable Company - *Toward an Integrated Bottom line pg 15*

[96] Laszlo .Chris (2003) - The Sustainable Company, *The Stakeholder Mind-set and Culture-pg45*

Business needs to identify and prioritise all key publics that directly or indirectly impact business performance from a materiality perspective. Once this is done, they need to be engaged by

- **explanation** of the sustainability vision and strategy
- **expectation clarity** of what is to be expected and delivered
- **engaging** all key stakeholders to give input and critique the strategy; sharing results transparently and building partnerships are a key step in stakeholder engagement

In most organisations, this is the responsibility of the PR/publicity and communication teams, and it shouldn't be so. Any organisation committed to sustainability must have its top team engaging with all strategic stakeholders and winning their commitment and support. Many leading apparel and footwear brands, e.g., Gap, Inc. and Nike have paid the price for not engaging with the key supply-chain stakeholders, only to be 'found out'.

The potential risk and damage to its corporate reputation is not worth the risk. Stakeholders must be viewed as a key feedback mechanism to improve the business, not just a 'supplier' who needs to be exploited.

As Christina Figueres, executive secretary of the UN Framework Convention on Climate Change (UNFCCC) mentions, 'If there is one thing that climate change teaches us, it is that we cannot prosper in isolation. No one country can ignore atmospheric science or the reality that our collective greenhouse gas emissions will dictate whether or not we risk tipping the world towards dangerous climate change.'[97]

The same is true for every business. They cannot ignore stakeholders and externalities any more. No business can win in isolation. The need to engage with supply chains, no matter which country they operate in, to ensure their commitment to the organisation's vision/sustainability strategy is key to its credibility and license to operate. In recent times, Unilever, Wal-Mart, IKEA, and M&S have used their global scale to get their many supply-chain partners to embrace sustainability and fall in line with their vision.

The recent Carbon Disclosure Project (CDP) report on country comparisons of supply-chain sustainability 2014-15 developed on behalf of CDP by Accenture highlights some of the key challenges.[98]

In the future, *managing supply-chain risk will be the deciding factor between success and failure.* Supply chains based in the United States, China, and Italy are considered vulnerable. India, China, and Brazil are mentioned as not doing enough to manage climate change.

Today, global business depends on China as the key manufacturing location of their supply chain. However, climate-change risks, especially scarce water resources, could significantly impact them. Organisations that do not mitigate this risk and develop less-vulnerable options could be out of business.

---

[97] Forward in Supply Chain Sustainability Revealed: A Country Comparison supply chain reports 2014-15 pp3

[98] Carbon Disclosure Project /Accenture report: Supply Chain Sustainability Revealed:
A Country Comparison supply chain reports 2014-15

4.6.1 Coalitions for Credibility

Identification of key stakeholders within its sphere of influence should be done after a systematic review considering the long-term strategy. Strategic partnerships should be formed with them, as many key MNCs have done, such as Unilever, Rainforest Alliance, and World Wildlife Fund. They become a credible source to position the companies' sustainability initiatives in the public domain. This is a more credible approach than a company advertising its responsible actions.

Let Credible Organisations Tell Your Story

Forming linkages with business schools and getting them to develop case studies is another approach to getting a company's story known and heard. Regular stakeholder feedback will circumvent the risk to corporate reputation. No business can have all the knowledge and expertise in all matters within its sphere of influence. Engaging strategic partners who have R&D expertise, such as universities and research institutes, will enhance its capabilities. Whilst stakeholder feedback and engagement can help business take timely action, ignoring them could be detrimental to its license to operate and corporate reputation. Tata learnt this the hard way with Tata Nano.

Business needs to proactively identify stakeholders and engage with them on potential risks and opportunities. It should be done in an ongoing and timely manner, especially if any one of the stakeholders has a direct impact on its business model and materiality. The top team needs to participate in the stakeholder engagement processes and not relegate it to a junior team that cannot take key decisions when required.

What Will Not Help?

- green wash sustainability reports with PR/publicity to win the consumer
- sustainability reports with no sustainability measures or trend data
- compliance-motivated tick-in-the-box actions
- not reporting a crisis
- the top team not being held accountable for the report
- not reporting all externalities and impacts

What Is Needed?

- commitment from the CEO to the frontline team to measure and report
- board focus and priority to review key SBPIs each month/quarter
- commitment to transparency and timely reporting
- engagement of stakeholders to review results
- building strategic coalitions of credibility
- making sustainability measurement and reporting mandatory

> **Strategic Corporate Sustainability - The Triple Bottom Line**
>
> **Strategic Stakeholder Engagement**
>
> Strategic stakeholder identification and engagement will be critical for every business to secure current and future business. Creating coalitions for credibility amongst stakeholders will consolidate a business by strengthening its licence to operate and its credibility. Managing supply-chain risks jointly with stakeholders will be crucial to all businesses.
>
> Business should impact its sphere of influence regarding all stakeholders, to move towards sustainability; this includes its employees.

4.7) Seventh Imperative

Sustainability-Led Differentiation and Innovation

The most compelling and powerful reason all businesses should pursue sustainability is the business opportunity it presents. The FT headline of 24 November 2014 stated 'The next generation of opportunities is sustainable and story led'. We could refer to them as blue oceans of green spaces. Sustainable innovation/R&D will be at the heart of future growth as we move towards a green economy. Business urgently needs to reinvent itself to be strategically relevant in a world that has been fostering short-term, unsustainable products and services.

The opportunity is to invest in sustainable innovation to create blue ocean market spaces, to replace all existing unsustainable ones. Business should seize the moment and create sustainable value for all stakeholders. One could say that the world needs to reinvent itself, and business needs to be the key driver.

4.7.1 Creating Blue Oceans of Green Market Spaces

The status quo presents an opportunity for all businesses to look at the marketplace and ask, how many of the current products and services are sustainably sourced, made, and distributed? Chances are, the majority do not make the cut. Business can identify them and create a sustainable substitute, which opens up a new blue ocean market space.

Sustainable investment has risen in 2014 to US$21.4 trillion from US$13.3 trillion in 2013, as per the Global Sustainable Investment Association (GSIA) with the United States, Canada, and Europe accounting for 99 per cent of global sustainable socially responsible investment (SRI) investing. An irreversible trend towards sustainable innovation and responsible investment is already in place.

Striving to reduce an individual product's ecological, water, and carbon footprint without losing the value it delivers is the challenge. Unilever, Wal-Mart, Interface, Patagonia, and Puma strive to do so in terms of each of the brands and products in their portfolios, and this concept is gaining traction amongst enlightened companies. The concept of carbon-neutral business with zero landfill should be an aspiration all enlightened, sustainability-driven companies strive for, by ensuring a seamless cradle-to-cradle transition of all resources being extracted from the planet.

Regeneration of extracted resources will be the next frontier of responsibility for all sustainable businesses. For too long, the stewardship of natural resources has been absent in most businesses, and all too often a readiness to send products to landfill for the slightest excuse confirms a false belief that resources are unlimited. This has led to unsustainable resource utilisation at high cost. Sustainable innovation should focus on creating strategic value to consumers and not contributing to the short-term throwaway culture. Every new product and service should strive to provide a significantly more sustainable solution than the previous option. Today we live in the 'fossil-fuel age of wasteful consumption' that needs to move to the 'age of responsible, sharing, and sustainable consumption'.

Many strategists believe that organisations should make a choice between differentiation and low cost, except for blue ocean strategy.[99] Creating new, uncontested market spaces that did not exist before at low cost and high value is the blue ocean paradigm, by pursuing differentiation and low cost simultaneously. Every new green solution that replaces an unsustainable current solution is poised to create a new blue ocean green market space. The reason blue ocean thinking is relevant in today's marketplace is that in the past, many of the green solutions were high cost and high value. This prevented many of those solutions from ever seeing the light of day. Mass adoption could never happen, and they remained niche markets at best. Blue ocean strategy focuses on low-cost solutions that have significantly higher value to the user. If the solution meets the blue ocean criteria and

---

[99]   Blue Ocean Strategy (2005) *https://hbr.org/2004/10/blue-ocean-strategy/ ar/1*

delivers sustainability as well, then we create a triple benefit: *low cost, high value, and sustainability.* If we approach sustainability challenges from the perspective of creating high sustainable value at lower cost in an innovative and creative manner, we create new blue oceans of green market spaces. The need for sustainability-led differentiation and innovation has been further espoused by the following individuals.

- Nidumolu, Prahalad and Rangeswari (2009),[100] Lubin and Esty (2010)[101] all refer to the opportunity for organisations to drive sustainable innovation and creating new market spaces for products and services to exploit the megatrend for sustainable differentiation.
- Lubin and Esty (2010) suggest 'sustainability-led differentiation' as a way to respond to the challenge of sustainability and identify it as an emerging challenge that needs a response.
- Strategic Corporate sustainability, Fernando (2010).[102] The concept I espoused at Cambridge 2007-14 was clear on the need for sustainability-led differentiation.

'A commitment to implementing strategies for sustainable business which **differentiates the organisation**, whilst impacting all stakeholders which are in its sphere of influence.'

---

[100] Nidumolu, R, Prahalad. C.K and Rangaswami.M.R (2009), Why Sustainability is now the key driver of innovation HBR September 2009 pp. 55-61

[101] Lubin.D.A and Esty.D.C (2010) The Sustainability Imperative-Lessons from leaders from previous game changing megatrends

[102] Fernando. Ravi (2012), "Sustainable globalization and Implications for strategic corporate and national sustainability", Corporate Governance, Vol.12 Issue: 4:579-589

This is an emerging paradigm where organisations embed sustainability in corporate strategy whilst differentiating on a sustainability paradigm.

Never has the opportunity to reinvent, redesign, and relaunch sustainable options been greater. Many an enlightened business is striving to create sustainable solutions delivering high value at low cost to create new green, uncontested market spaces.

The following are examples of business initiatives that have done so by committing to strategic corporate sustainability by differentiating and innovating on a sustainability platform.

- The Body Shop: **No animal testing.** *Created a new paradigm in the cosmetic market for low-cost (eliminated high packaging costs), sustainable, and high-quality products.*
- Unilever: **Sustainable living plan.** *This one strategy guides every step the organisation takes and has energised all employees.*
- General Electric: **Ecomagination.** *Set a new global benchmark for sustainable engineering, design, and resource utilisation.*
- Toyota: **Hybrid cars.**[103] *Created a new paradigm away from 100 per cent fossil-fuel-driven automobiles.*
- M&S: **Plan A.**[104] *Set the benchmark for sustainable retailing.*
- Accor Hotels: **Planet 21.** *Sets the standard for sustainable hospitality.*
- TESLA: **Electric cars.**[105] *Created a new market space for 100 per cent fossil-fuel-free automobiles and home solar.*

---

[103] Toyota Hybrid cars - *www.toyota.com/hybrid-cars*
[104] Marks and Spencer Plan A- *planareport.marksandspencer.com*
[105] Tesla Motors - *www.teslamotors.com*

- Interface: **Sustainable carpeting.** *Set the global benchmark for sustainable and practical carpeting.*
- Wal-Mart: **Sustainability 360.** *Set a global benchmark for sustainability impact across its supply chain.*
- Puma: **Environmental P&L.** *Set a new benchmark for costing externalities.*
- Women **Go Beyond:**[106] *Set a new paradigm for social sustainability-led differentiation and women's empowerment in the apparel sector.*
- **A Home for Every Plantation Worker:**[107] *Set a new benchmark for social sustainability in the plantation sector by making the livelihood of plantation worker the differentiator.*

Each of the above organisations has created blue oceans of new green, uncontested market spaces by differentiating its products on a sustainability paradigm. It requires CEOs, boards, and strategists with a sustainability mindset to create such opportunities. An appreciation of the irreversible trajectory of sustainability and the opportunity it presents is the prerequisite.

The reality is that a majority of businesses languish in red oceans of unsustainable products and services, racing to the bottom on price to retain the consumer. This is a recipe for disaster, as many companies have found out and will find out in the future, as they did not embrace the impending change in

---

[106] INSEAD Case 2006 'Strategic corporate social responsibility in the Apparel industry'
INSEAD Case 2008 'Leveraging Corporate Responsibility'
[107] INSEAD Case 2009 'Mabroc Kelani Valley - Creating the Ethical Tea brand of the World'

time. Creating blue oceans of green market spaces requires a systematic, step-by-step approach as follows.

Step 1 - A Vision for Sustainability with One Strategy

The CEO and the board must set a clear vision for the organisation to take a position in the emerging green economy by leveraging its competencies and acquiring skills where necessary to do so. It will be essential for the organisation to commit to strategic corporate sustainability and mobilise the seven imperatives mentioned earlier. The vision should articulate the green market space it intends to dominate and what goals and milestones it wants to achieve and when. Ideally the vision should galvanise the organisation and inspire all stakeholders to pursue it.

Step 2 - Review the Existing Portfolio to Develop the 'As-Is'[108] Strategy Canvas.

The review of the existing portfolio through the prism of sustainability is the next step. This key step will highlight the 'as-is' position of the product or service from a sustainability/ key value factors of the market perspective. Thereafter, it should direct the business as to what needs to be done to convert an existing product operating in a red ocean of competition to create a new sustainable, low-cost option. The ERRC grid[109] could be used to identify what value factors and current product service elements need to be changed.

---

[108] ©Chan.Kim & Mauborgne 'As Is' Strategy Canvas - Blue Ocean strategy (2005) pg.23-44

[109] © Chan. Kim & Mauborgne ERRC Grid - Blue Ocean Strategy (2005) pg.35

- **Eliminate and Reduce** - Identify market value factors and key product/service elements that need to be eliminated and reduced from the current product portfolio, as they do not conform to the principles of sustainability or blue ocean strategy.

This key step is to establish the unsustainable aspects or elements of the product and its supply chain. In addition, the **materiality** of all external and internal risks faced by the business that have the greatest potential to disrupt the business model need to be identified in the 'as-is' canvas to determine the key priorities that need to be addressed in the risk-mitigation strategy.

A critical in-depth analysis of the products and services to establish its current credentials from the perspective of sustainability is an essential step to map out the as-is situation. For example, a detailed breakdown of every element, from its product formulation to its packaging, will help establish if the raw materials or ingredients used are sustainably sourced and manufactured.

Is the packaging sustainably sourced? Is current supply chain and logistics -transport and distribution sustainable?

The results should prompt the business to establish what could be done to ensure each element is improved, to develop the 'to-be' strategy canvas towards creating a sustainable product or service. Blue ocean strategy is an excellent approach to review the existing portfolio and create a new, more sustainable portfolio using the 'as-is' and 'to-be' strategy canvases for both the industry and current products and services.

The review will prompt many questions: Can we relaunch our existing portfolio, or do we need to create a new portfolio? Can they be made at lower cost but create significantly higher sustainable value to the end customer? Do we need to redesign our range?

The organisation will identify new product opportunities as it takes this disciplined approach by market or industry. The challenge is to create a market space that will deliver the end consumer/customer a superior need solution at a lower cost - and most importantly from the perspective of sustainability. Both functional and emotional elements can be reviewed to identify elements that will create greater sustainable value at a lower cost.

Step 3 - Create and Implement the 'To-Be'[110] Strategy Canvas

As business critically scans the market, another key tool that can guide this exercise is the blue oceans strategy *six paths framework,*[111] Path 6 - Time - an irreversible trajectory and trend that provides forward-thinking businesses the opportunity to create a new blue ocean market space. The many opportunities for sustainable products and services will emerge as most existing products have been developed with little or no consideration to sustainability. The majority of today's products and services

---

[110] © Chan.Kim & Mauborgne 'To be' Strategy Canvas - Blue Ocean strategy (2005) pg.23-44

[111] © Chan.Kim & Mauborgne 'Six paths framework' - Blue Ocean strategy (2005) pg.47-80

are unsustainable and operate in crowded red oceans. This gives rise to the opportunity to recreate, reinvent, redesign, and relaunch sustainable options and create new green market space. The organisation could form a multifunctional team to scan the market's emerging needs, to anticipate sustainable consumption needs.

In addition, it should pay special attention to nonusers of the products or services, to create new blue ocean opportunities to attract them into the market. This key step requires market intelligence with a vision and commitment to sustainability to be able to identify and anticipate the emerging new opportunities for new market spaces.

The next step is to create the to-be strategy canvas based on the findings. The many possibilities that emerge from this exercise need to be fine-tuned based on the prism of creating sustainable value for the customers and consumers. This exercise in value analysis will highlight those elements, processes, or factors that need to be replaced at low cost but will not diminish the value they create for the end user.

The goal is to create greater sustainable value at lower cost. The blue ocean strategy[112] ERRC grid (eliminate, reduce, raise, and create) should be used at this stage.

---

[112] Chan Kim .W and Mauborgne. R- Blue Ocean strategy – How to Create Uncontested Market Spaces and Make the Competition irrelevant, © 2015 Harvard Business School Publishing Corporation

- **Raise and Create** – What elements need to be raised from
  a sustainability perspective (e.g., sustainable new-product
  formats and sourcing), and which new elements need to be
  created so that a new blue ocean sustainable market space
  can be created?

The **materiality analysis** done in the as-is strategy canvas
will need to be addressed comprehensively to mitigate risk by
eliminating or reducing the identified risks in the to-be strategy
canvas by raising and creating new approaches and solutions. The
sustainability mindset leader will challenge the as-is red ocean
status quo and set the stage for creating the to-be blue ocean
green market space. The end result will be the identification of
new green, uncontested market spaces that make today's red
ocean unsustainable competitive markets irrelevant. It could
necessitate redesigning the product with sustainably sourced basic
raw materials, the creation of new sustainability-led innovation,
and establishing a new more planet-friendly sourcing and supply-
chain strategy.

Anticipating what new products and services could be required
in the future based on some of the emerging sustainability
challenges could be another opportunity for an entrée to create a
new green market space, e.g., water scarcity and clean air. Both
these approaches will require a strategic approach to investment
that will create new opportunities within its current portfolio
and unlock new green market spaces altogether. A short list
of possible product or service configurations, price points, and
market potential will emerge. The final product or service options
must either leverage the organisation's existing competences or

identify and acquire new competencies to seize the opportunity. They must be low-cost options with the potential to create high sustainable value. The final list will go through the process of CEO/board approval to sanction the investment and R&D alignment to create a new green market space.

The HBR (December 2014) titled 'What Frugal Innovators Do'[113] refers to the need for building circular value networks. It states:

> most companies today operate linear value chains in which products are designed, produced, sold and consumed and end up in landfills, this linear economic model is wasteful, costly and environmentally unsustainable. Instead to be resource-efficient, CEOs must reinvent their value chains to operate in a circular way by embracing sustainable methods of design (like cradle to cradle (C2C) and production and distribution (like industrial symbiosis).These circular economy techniques enable the continual reuse of materials, parts and components and even waste.

Step 4 - Test Market and Launch One Strategy

The one strategy must then invest to create the new sustainable market opportunities. From the to-be strategy canvas will emerge a potential sustainability-led differentiator. The organisation will need to invest in the identified differentiator to raise and create it to be the one that unlocks the blue ocean market space.

---

[113] Radjou. N and Prabu .J (HBR December 2014) 'What Frugal Innovators Do'

Once this has been identified, the consumer needs to be made aware of the more sustainable option that is lower cost but will create greater value. Building a strong coalition for credibility to endorse, communicate, and position the new offering is a key low-cost initiative to establish a brand in the new green market space, in much the same way Tesla has invested to secure the emerging electric vehicle market space by developing advanced robotic manufacture, a charging-station network, and battery-manufacturing plants. This is a case in point of how to invest to unlock the future potential.

The strategy must also review the entire supply chain to ensure it can stand up to the promise made by the new sustainability-led differentiator. Every potential gap must be evaluated to circumvent any activist claim that invalidates the strategy. Getting supply-chain partners committed to the strategy is a key alignment that must happen prior to its final launch using fair process.

A test market is recommended in a strong market where conversion or adoption is to be expected. It is also prudent to do so in a complex market where high resistance is expected. The test market should be run over a period of time that gives the organisation adequate opportunity to learn from both and fine-tune its strategy. As many have found out, what is rationally expected does not always happen in the marketplace. The final optimum strategy needs to be put to the test *prior* to going national, regional, or global, to fine-tune the one sustainable corporate strategy.

Step 5 - Recreating New Blue Oceans of Green Market Spaces

As a business creates a new blue ocean market space, if it is a unique and lucrative opportunity, the competition will enter. Most times, the first mover will have a three- to seven-year window depending on the complexity and investment made, to secure the leadership position, after which time it will attract a host of competitors who will turn the new blue ocean market space into a crowded red ocean. Every blue ocean will turn red over time.

The best defence is to attack oneself with superior offerings and create another new market space. To do so, a commitment to investment in continuous sustainability-led innovation and differentiation to initiate the next phase of research and development must also be put in place, to keep the differentiator relevant, strategic, and sustainable. Ideally, an innovation pipeline must continuously flow, as each new green ocean attracts competition and turns red. To stand still is to be overtaken.

Once a new green market space has been created, the organisation must constantly challenge itself to keep recreating new blue oceans of green market spaces by ensuring creativity, innovation, and technology play their roles. Today the opportunity for green innovation is limitless, from smart scooters to electronic undershoes, e-mobility of the masses, wearable environmental monitors, portable solar charges, and smart and connected homes.

The recommended approach is to set up two independent teams within the business-development and innovation division to review the consumer or customer need currently being met from two independent perspectives as follows:

- Assemble a team to review the current offering and potential future need from a sustainability perspective and create new options to do so sustainably.
- Assemble a team to review the marketplace from a blue ocean strategy perspective, using the tools to establish if a new market space can be created.
- After doing so independently, the teams can come together and now create a new blue ocean market space that is sustainable.

The established business will always find it difficult to abandon or even consider departing from successful unsustainable products and services infrastructure and investments that have sustained them to date.

Industry after industry, business after business remains caught in the red ocean trap of unsustainable products – fossil fuels, tobacco, carbonated soft drinks. In recent times, a few business leaders and entrepreneurs have created new green market spaces, and the examples keep mounting each day.

Tesla Electric Vehicles invested in the required sustainability-led innovation, infrastructure, and the world's largest EV battery facilities ahead of GM, which mothballed its EV due to the oil lobby. Toyota, which first recognised the need for hybrids, is now on the path to create hydrogen-cell vehicles. Tesla and Toyota have led the way, leaving Mercedes, Volkswagen, BMW, Nissan,

Hyundai, Ford, and GM all following a global tipping point for EVs and a new green market space.

Airbnb leveraged the emerging trend of the sharing economy. The organisation is leading the way by leveraging rooms in existing homes around the world as a low-cost, high-value option to hotel rooms. The company sold more rooms than the established Hilton chain of hotels in 2014, and its market capitalisation is significantly higher than that of Hyatt.

Both Tesla and Airbnb have created new market spaces in established markets, beating all the established market leaders by creating a blue ocean in a sustainability-oriented and differentiated way. This confirms the opportunity for any sustainability-driven start-up to challenge the well-established, cash-rich market leaders by outmanoeuvring the existing business model. All businesses must embrace the brave new world of sustainable solutions and invest to create new green, uncontested market spaces that will accelerate once each nation commits to the new sustainable-development goals in November 2015. The opportunity is restricted only by our imagination.

4.7.2 Sustainable Innovation/R&D

Global R&D spending increased from US$760 billion in 2001 to US$1,430 billion by 2011.The new frontier of sustainable innovation, R&D will account for a greater share of this in the next decade as business after business begins to see the opportunity of creating new sustainable products and services.

The Arthur D. Little Report (2004),[114] defined sustainable innovation as the 'creation of new market spaces, products and services or processes driven by social and environmental sustainability issues'.

A survey amongst eighty companies by both the World Business Council for Sustainable Development and Arthur D. Little indicated that 95 per cent of companies believe that sustainability-driven innovation has the potential to bring business value. Almost a quarter believe that it will definitely deliver business value, and 60 per cent of companies see potential benefits to their top line, whilst 43 per cent see further benefits to the bottom line. Creating a new sustainability-led strategic differentiator will be the inspiration for innovation and R&D investment. When business selects the sustainability-led differentiator, it is already on the journey to creating a new green market space for its product or service. As business makes the transition towards one strategy by mainstreaming sustainability, its investment will be focused on sustainable innovation and creating strategic differentiators it can own and leverage.

Nike's Hannah Jones VP –Sustainability and CEO Mark Parker are driving the sustainability agenda by taking bold steps to create new market spaces.

> Integrating sustainability is not just a good opportunity for business. It is essential for success in a world of constrained resources. Right now every

---

[114] Little. D. A 2005 How leading companies are using sustainability - driven innovation to win Tomorrow's Customers © 2005 Arthur D. Little

business has a choice to make. We choose to move fast, using sustainability as a force for innovation. We choose to embrace transparency, collaboration and advocacy as tools to unlock opportunity and enable us to thrive in a clean and green economy.
—Mark Parker, CEO and president, Nike

Economic sustainability is the hygiene factor that gets businesses into the race, and unlike in the past, operational efficiency will not set any organisation apart. Increasingly, the two sustainability elements that will drive differentiation and innovation are environmental or social sustainability.

Every business needs to identify the key sustainability issues that are relevant and material to its survival and growth. These issues will then be the sustainable business performance indicators (SBPIs) that guide the business and drive its sustainability strategy. Business must invest on creating differentiators that help create market spaces that exist today and will emerge in the future. As we hurtle towards a planet without the very basic resources for life - water and clean air, as highlighted in the first chapter - there is an urgent need for a new global model for sustainable business, where sustainable resource utilisation and consumption are mandatory and not optional. This presents business blue oceans of opportunity to create new green market spaces that make the competition irrelevant.

What Will Not Help?
- going green for a niche and continuing with an unsustainable range
- making unsubstantiated sustainability claims

- not investing in innovation/R&D to retain the differentiator
- not collaborating with universities and research institutes for inspiration
- creating high-cost sustainable solutions that cannot be afforded

What Is Needed?

- a belief that strategic corporate sustainability is the *only* way forwards
- a commitment to the one strategy focused on creating sustainable value
- an investment in innovation and R&D to search for sustainable solutions
- a commitment to creating blue oceans of green market spaces in a red ocean of unsustainable products
- a commitment to sustainability-led differentiation and innovation

Strategic Corporate Sustainability - The Triple Bottom Line

Sustainability-Led Innovation and Differentiation

Investing in sustainable innovation and R&D to create sustainability-led differentiators will unlock many blue oceans of green market spaces. Creating new green market spaces has to be the focus of all business, as it's the greatest opportunity in a world full of unsustainable products and services operating in red ocean markets. Critically examining all existing products and services *through the prism of sustainability* will highlight the opportunity to launch sustainable offerings to create new green market spaces. Commitment to continuous improvement to raise and create new green market spaces and recreate the offering to be even more sustainable is a journey with no destination.

CHAPTER 5

The Future
A Call to Action
for a Sustainable Planet!

5.1 Introduction

The time has come to move from words, commitments, and pledges to urgent action. The world has taken little concrete action to match its abundance of reports and words. As the planet hurtles towards chaos, the last chapter is an urgent call to action for a sustainable planet. We need business leaders setting the pace and nudging all national leaders to act urgently on climate change.

The final chapter is in two parts as follows.

Part 1. Strategic Corporate Sustainability focuses on issues that support the strategic institutionalisation of sustainability in business. The need for a stewardship role is highlighted with the mobilisation of the mandatory environmental strategy with SBPI (sustainable business performance indicators) that track its progress towards carbon neutrality. Eight initiatives have been identified for business to facilitate systemic change to the prevailing status quo.

Part 2. Strategic National Sustainability focuses on nine macro issues that need to be addressed with urgency as a step towards institutionalising sustainability in the public sector. They cover an imperative for sustainable resource utilisation and mandatory NSPI (national sustainability performance indicators) that stem from the UNSDGs to track progress. In each case, the key role business needs to play is outlined. In both cases, the need for business to form strategic partnerships with the public sector to address the new UN sustainable development goals is emphasised. The chapter ends with a call to action for a sustainable planet.

5.2 Part 1 - Strategic Corporate Sustainability

The Future Sustainable Corporation and Sustainable Business Performance Indicators (SBPIs). The future sustainable corporation will need to have twin focuses:

a) developing a sustainable business model for its entire business

b) being accountable for reducing the carbon footprint in its sphere of influence with an environmental strategy tracked by SBPIs, e.g., ecological, carbon, water, employee, and end consumers' footprint as a result of the company portfolio and supply chain, etc.

Securing sustainable energy/resource needs will be a key initiative that every business must invest in, for example, renewable energy, water resources, and all key natural and processed resources that form a part of its portfolio.

Forming collaborations and partnerships that secure them will be the way forwards, as is the case with Apple and Google with solar and wind energy. Every key resource business requires for its existence and growth will need to be sustainably secured in a manner that supports its regeneration. The future corporation will not depend on governments to do so, nor will it leave things to chance based on the current models of access.

The following SBPIs are an example of what the checklist could cover.

- sustainable product portfolio
- sustainable renewable energy
- carbon-neutral business – zero landfill
- sustainable water/resource management and regeneration
- employee sustainability – housing and energy
- sustainable supply chains of all key raw-material resources
- sustainable R&D and innovation Investment
- conversion to smart and green technologies
- sustainable governance measures
- GRI sustainability measurement and reporting

Each business needs to identify those key SBPIs relevant to its business and industry.

A New Mandate for Sustainable Business

Business needs to embrace strategic corporate sustainability and influence national policy to change the landscape for sustainable business. Today, the lack of policies and strategies creates an uneven playing field for businesses aspiring to do so. The current cost of doing business sustainably is higher than that of doing business unsustainably. This is due to many unsustainable practices business currently employs to lower costs, such as environmental pollution, child labour, compromise on banned substances, etc. The moment new legislation comes into play whereby all business has to play by the same sustainable business rulebook, the cost of doing business will be the same.

Currently, many enlightened businesses are disadvantaged for doing the right thing, as there is no level playing field, and too many get away with doing the wrong thing! The key beneficiary of business striving for sustainability is the consumer, who will initially pay the real cost of all resources and thereafter accept that these costs will reduce as business is incentivised to innovate sustainably and create mass-market solutions. Any business committed to sustainable business needs to commit to this approach, irrespective of the industry it operates in if global sustainability is to be achieved.

Global Coalitions for Collaboration

Every nation and business must be challenged to form coalitions and partnerships for strategic impact and credibility. Today, most nations and corporations lack both the credibility and the technical knowledge to achieve strategic sustainability goals on their own. Impact can be achieved through forming collaborations across industries to solve common issues. Collaborations that leverage R&D and innovation are another frontier. Credibility can be achieved with transparency and partnerships with organisations that have, over the years, established credibility.

Creating an ecosystem for such collaboration will break down national, regional, and single-business boundaries and leverage the global talent pool to resolve all sustainability challenges. Intellectual Ventures (USA) has done so by moving from the previous 'power of one' to the 'power of many' to address all global challenges forming linkages and collaborative agreements globally.

Credibility is the basis on which global, regional, and local acceptance and license to operate are achieved. Organisations like the UN Global Compact, WBCSD (World Business Council for Sustainable Development), WWF (World Wildlife Fund), Greenpeace, Rainforest Alliance, Forest Stewardship Council, Habitat for Humanity, World Vision, CERES, and Plan B Corporations give business legitimacy and credibility as they partner with them.

Collaboration within and across industry is required to minimise unsustainable resource utilisation. The future is for global collaboration, where nations advanced in sustainability will collaborate with nations that need technological support; where businesses, NGOs, and nations all work together for the sustainability of the one planet we have.

Business-Led Sustainability Education
Creating a planet where all human beings are educated of the need for sustainability and stewardship of resources must pervade every nation.

Business can play a pivotal role to instil simple concepts like these:

All resources are limited. Nature sustains humanity. Waste needs to be minimised and eliminated. Forests and biodiversity need to be protected. Every drop of fresh water is precious. The sharing economy minimises waste. Ownership of all goods is unnecessary. Respect for all humanity, irrespective of race, colour, or beliefs, is crucial for a sustainable world.

These concepts could be sponsored by leading MNCs and local businesses so that they could be introduced from Montessori or kindergarten to university for sustaining the planet. Today, with mobile technology and the Internet, this could be achieved in whatever language needed in record time. Those in mainstream media, social media, graphic design, and education should see this as an urgent challenge and contribute their expertise. Even the illiterate understand images and pictures.

Sustainability 101 must be mandatory for all leaders of nations, businesses, or positions of responsibility that impact the use of the planet's resources. The planet has hope if we embrace and embed this concept across humanity. The planet can no longer have climate deniers, strong oil lobbies, and sustainability-stalling interest groups delay any urgent action needed for the planet's sustainability. This science-defying movement has delayed and stalled the urgent policy legislation needed to address the planet's most pressing sustainability challenges, which were clearly highlighted as far back as 1987 in the landmark report, 'Our Common Future'. Not only has the anti-sustainability lobby been able to stall urgent action, but the industries funding it have also accelerated the decimation of natural resources and use of fossil fuels at an unprecedented rate in the past thirty years, to quadruple nominal global world product through accelerated resource utilisation and waste. A tipping point for sustainability will be achieved when the existence and influence of such lobby groups to harm the planet must be legally made impossible. After all, we are talking of meeting the needs of future generations and the stewardship of our one planet's resources. Regeneration and not exploitation should be the new paradigm to manage all natural resources.

Waste, especially of agricultural produce and food, should not have any place if humanity is to adopt this new posture. We keep clearing forest after forest on the pretext that we have a world that needs to be fed and then send 40 per cent back to landfill? How can that make any sense?

Business-Led, Sustainable Consumption

If the majority of business embraces strategic corporate sustainability, then a significant percentage of products and services will be sustainably sourced, made, and distributed. Every consumer must be made aware of the current waste culture that prevails, wherein between 30 and 40 per cent of extracted and processed natural resources end up in landfill. Business must lead the way by managing its supply chains and high inventories to minimise the potential for waste. The need for adopting sustainable lifestyles should be made mandatory communication in every pack. The sustainable choices available must be made known to every consumer to meet their needs and wants using mobile and Internet technology, whereby every time a consumer reaches for a product or service, he or she could reach for the sustainable option, which highlights its carbon and water footprint.

New sustainable lifestyle-enabling apps that let the consumer know in real time the most sustainable option available should be part and parcel of every new smart phone. These sustainable apps need to advise consumers of unhealthy air- and water pollution levels, expired and unsuitable food (E. coli and salmonella), health vital signs, energy consumption, and sustainable energy use. The sharing economy options need to be scaled up for every durable product or service and sustainable consumption, enabling information need to be at the tip of the finger and the touch of a button in a planet that will have more smart phones than people. Making informed decisions to purchase or hire the sustainable option every time has to be made the norm. Today, with the exception of a few advanced nations and a few product categories, we are all contributing to unsustainable consumption.

Every urban home must be installed with advanced technology to control the efficient utilisation of all utilities as mandatory, not optional – electricity, water, etc. China's 'No Roof Left Behind' programme should be a global programme, and nations should be measured and rewarded for installing solar energy. Unsustainable consumption and unsustainable resource utilisation need to be exposed in real time in the case of nations and businesses, and they must be held responsible. Technology needs to be mobilised to achieve this end. The polluter pays principal needs to be enforced with the required government legislation in place.

Business Empowering Women to Go Beyond[115]

Women in most nations are marginalised, disadvantaged, and not engaged in the global economy. Though women play a significant role in key sectors and industries that contribute to economic growth, e.g., apparel, plantations, and electronic

---

[115] INSEAD Cases 'MAS Holdings: Strategic Corporate Social Responsibility in the Apparel Industry (ECCH 2006) and MAS Holdings: Strategic Corporate Social Responsibility in the Apparel Industry (ECCH 2009) for the 'Women Go beyond' concept

assembly in nations that form a key part of the global supply chain, they are exploited. Archaic and exploitative policies need to be revamped by business that is supported by such supply chains. Today, women are stigmatised, poorly compensated, and exploited in most nations. Future global sustainability requires women to be equally engaged and incentivised to play a key role.

Gender diversity needs to populate corporate boards and all key strategy-formulation bodies to bring about greater sensitivity to social and environmental reality than their male counterparts.

Disincentive for Wealth and Influence Beyond a Point

The power and influence of business needs to be channelled and refocused for sustainability. The disproportionate influence among a few large corporations and nations on how natural resources are utilised and deployed needs to be eliminated. Today, capitalism perpetuates a system where the rich get richer at the expense of the poor; 85,000 of the richest people on the planet have access to more wealth than the combined wealth of 3.5 billion of the world's population. MNCs, which have plundered the resources of poor nations and continents, *must* be held accountable to compensate these nations at the current value of resources towards the sustainable development of the exploited nation. Africa, Asia, and Latin America will be key beneficiaries. A new taxation regime, which is a disincentive for accessing wealth beyond a point with no tax loopholes, needs to be mainstreamed.

Business, Generation Y, and Millennials

Generation Y and millennials need to have a voice in the way resource utilisation takes place, to ensure their needs are not compromised in the future. They need to be informed and empowered in real time to halt the potential impacts of unsustainable choices and have the voice and platform to do so. Business can take the lead to empower future generations by creating such a platform in universities and high schools that gives generation Y and millennial youth an opportunity to influence business decisions. They need to be enlightened and educated of the challenges the planet faces and the right they have to demand stewardship of the planet's resources from all leaders endowed with this responsibility. These steps will contribute to the stewardship of resources for all future generations.

These ideas need to be converted to strategic initiatives and action plans by enlightened business leaders, working together with NGOs which operate in that space.

5.2 Part 2 - Strategic National Sustainability

A Global and National Natural Resource Bank for Sustainable Resource Utilisation

The planet urgently needs a 'global natural resource bank' that keeps score of the rate at which limited natural resources are diminishing and informs all stakeholders in a timely manner to halt it. Key global agencies and nations such as UN, WRI, NASA, WWF, Conservation International, China, USA, EU, Russia, Brazil, Congo, Indonesia, and Malaysia should combine forces to enable and empower it. Its role will be to highlight and give visibility in real time to the extraction and pollution of resources, as well as to support the regeneration of resources. A snapshot of current and projected resources by nation will play a key role in alerting all leaders of the need for responsible and strategic resource utilisation from the perspective meeting needs of future generations. This needs to be complemented with a 'national natural resource bank', which has been empowered to implement a national resource utilisation strategy with integrity and a regeneration mindset.

The most valuable resources need to be focused upon. Halting deforestation and managing the risk of physical and economic water shortages projected to impact humanity by 2025 will need to be a key focus. Water-management strategies need to comprehensively cover rainwater harvesting, in addition to investment in the cleanup of all waterways, rivers, and the many polluted sources of water. Laws to stop the pollution of groundwater and aquifers need to be implemented. As water waste is rampant in many developed nations, targeted reduction of per-capita water consumption is another opportunity. The aggressive reduction of the water footprints of businesses and governments needs to be a key focus.

The same goes for forest cover and deforestation. Ideally this organisation should be given the mandate for influencing the sustainable management and stewardship of forest cover. Its key role will be to create awareness among decision-makers of the unsustainable resource utilisation in real time. Having lost 50 per cent of forest cover and 52 per cent of animal species in the last thirty years, can we take the risk of managing this precious resource the way we have in the past? If the current status quo continues, we risk zero forest cover, biodiversity, and animal species in the next thirty years.

If sustainable development requires us to leave any resources for future generations, then this initiative is the key.

Driving all business and nations to reforest garnering the investment needed by rechanneling subsidies for fossil fuels and deforestation will be their ambit. A halt to fossil-fuel exploration and retention of fossil-fuel reserves will need to be monitored as we move towards renewable energy. The need for wealth funds and all investments in fossil fuels to be divested and reinvested in renewable energy will contribute to ensuring the balance fossil fuels reserves remain where they are. The 'operate in isolation with an island mentality' that empowers nations and businesses to manage all resources in their sphere of influence has failed, as there is no global visibility if they are doing so. Resource utilisation, as a result, is far from sustainable; it's out of control.

This highlights the paucity of the current world order and crises we are all faced with because of an uncoordinated approach to managing global resource sustainability. Business needs to commit to strategic and sustainable resource utilisation and work closely with both the global and national 'natural resource banks' to do so. This could be a commitment all UN Global Compact signatories make, and thereafter it can be expanded to all listed companies as a prerequisite by global stock exchanges.

A Global Reward System for Sustainability

A new global, national, and business-level system that rewards strategic and sustainable decisions is a prerequisite for sustainable resource utilisation. The guiding principle is to reward the stewardship and sustainable utilisation of all resources. This should dissuade business leaders from implementing strategies that focus on growth at any cost. It should reward the strategic regeneration of every resource in the sphere of influence of business. This requires a strategic mind shift towards the sustainable stewardship of resources. This new system will immediately support the purpose of the national 'natural resource banks' in a significant way, as there will be an incentive for every business to do so. The reward structure must recognise those companies that have an excellent track record of doing so. They should be allocated more resources to continue to do so. Every business needs to give priority to the stewardship of resources.

Public-private partnerships can be empowered to jointly utilise resources to meet both the current and future needs of the nations. This is true especially for MNCs and transnationals that have a global ecological footprint and need to support sustainable development as the way forward for sustainable business.

A National Sustainability Commission

This requires reworking the mandate that political and business leaders have today. We need an independent national sustainability commission in every nation that audits initiatives and advises all parties of the strategic sustainable choices available. Each nation needs to install a national sustainability commission that is empowered and has the legitimacy to act as the guardians of national sustainability *beyond any term of office of any national leader or party*. The strategic sustainability of a nation must not be left to the whims and fancies of each government, political party, and leader's attitude to sustainability, but be held under the stewardship of the national sustainability commission. The commission should be empowered to track progress on NSPIs and all current and future investments in the nation, to ensure they are done sustainably.

National Sustainability Performance Indicators (NSPIs)

Government leaders must take ownership of creating sustainable nations by committing to deliver on the new sustainable development goals. Each nation needs to focus on those areas that are material and strategic to its future. The non-negotiable NSPIs for each nation implementing a strategic national sustainability policy and strategy should cover all the new UN sustainable development goals, for example:

- alleviating poverty and dismantling inequality
- reducing carbon emissions and pollution
- exiting fossil-fuel-based energy and eliminating subsides
- investing subsidies to scale up renewables with urgency
- ensuring sustainable utilisation and regeneration of resources
- halting deforestation and increasing 'green cover' through reforestation
- incentivising sustainable innovation
- driving and rewarding sustainable consumption lifestyles
- creating sustainable cities and food access within close proximity
- initiating stewardship of existing water resources and minimising waste and pollution
- reducing credit debt as a per cent of GDP to stop unsustainable consumption

The strategic national sustainability policy and strategy must be reviewed and evaluated by the independent national sustainability commission and corrective action taken regularly.

Green Energy

Fossil fuels need to be replaced 100 per cent by green and renewable energy, for a cleaner, greener, and healthier planet, with at least 80 per cent achieved by 2030. Business must lead the way by securing its energy requirements with 100 per cent renewable energy. The fastest-growing global economies like China, India, and Brazil are accelerating economic growth at any cost. This has resulted in these nations being the most polluted and unhealthy nations to live in.

Air and water pollution is causing unprecedented health crises. Every nation pursuing economic growth, ignoring environmental stewardship and social progress, needs to learn from the Chinese experience. Today, the cost of cleaning up the environment in China is estimated to be 6.5 per cent of GDP. The same is true for India, where 3 to 7 per cent of GDP will need to be inducted. Vietnam, Indonesia, and other populous nations will have to take note and change their current modus operandi.

Solving the energy crisis wherein we move away from fossil-fuel dependence will ensure global warming is halted and pollution is minimised. Programmes such as the 'No Roof Left Behind' campaign to leverage every roof for solar and incentives for an accelerated move to EV automobiles and all transportation will help solve the global energy challenge that will be the foundation for the green economy. Business needs to partner with governments in their attempt to do.

Sustainable Agriculture and Distribution

Humanity needs food, water, and clean air for survival. In the future, sustainable agricultural practices will need to replace the current unsustainable practices of soil degradation and unacceptable waste of agricultural produce, which varies from 30 to 40 per cent globally. Business needs to be engaged in eliminating this waste with new and sustainable supply-chain solutions. Urban agriculture; soil enrichment; and elimination of waste on distribution, packaging, and storage will need to be focused on. Sourcing of agricultural produce closer to where consumption will take place will minimise emissions. The reinvigoration of small and medium-scale community agriculture will ensure healthier and sustainable food for all.

Sustainable nanotechnology-led solutions should be inducted, to solve the global water, agriculture, and energy issues, and the two areas in which business collaboration can add significant value are in sustainable use of fertiliser and managing the supply chain to eliminate food waste. Waste of any resource is unacceptable in a resource-scarce planet, even more so if we strive to create a sustainable planet.

Sustainable Cities

Urbanisation projections show a migration towards 66 per cent of the global population living in urban cities by 2050. Urgent strategic sustainability planning needs to be initiated to meet the public transportation, water, sanitation, food, and energy needs, to cope with the emerging trend. The smart infrastructure required for sustainable cities of the future will need to be in place today if all needs are to be met in a sustainable way. Efficient green public transport should be the only option for most urban dwellers in the future. Ensuring green cover is maximised with vertical green cover and rooftop solar will need to be the norm. The business sector is best positioned to work with the public sector to create smart cities that manage resource utilisation and create sustainable solutions to address every single urban challenge from the perspective of good for the city, the business, and the nation.

Sustainable Tourism

Tourism is a force for good that needs to be harnessed for global sustainability. As the world's largest and most humanity-engaging industry, the global responsibility it can wield is immense if all tourists were enlightened of the need for stewardship of natural beauty. In 2014, more than 1 billion people engaged in tourism and travelled abroad. This figure is set to increase and has the potential to move up from one in every seven to one in four human beings in the next decade. The opportunity to educate every single global tourist and traveller on his or her stewardship role can ensure sustainable tourism can be a force for good. Sustainable tourism can impact societal and environmental issues of each community in a positive manner whilst contributing to the economy.

The World Tourism Organisation, working closely with regional and national tourism bodies, should inspire and enlist every single tourist to be committed to the sustainability of the planet.

Business needs to play the game-changing role by creating a new model for sustainable tourism. The Airbnb model of leveraging existing resources needs to be the priority, and conservation and regeneration can be the themes around which global tourists are engaged in a purposeful way.

Asian Sustainability

Asia holds the key to global sustainability, as most of the current and future economic powerhouses are located on that continent. China, India, Indonesia, and Vietnam, along with the established Asian leaders Japan, South Korea, Malaysia, Singapore, and Thailand, have the responsibility to recalibrate their focus from GDP growth to sustainable growth, to manage an unprecedented demand for resources to meet the needs and aspirations of their growing middle class. Other populous Asian nations like Bangladesh and Pakistan, along with emerging nations like Myanmar and Sri Lanka will need to do the same. The cost of providing energy and infrastructure, coupled with the need to address rising costs of climate change, inequality, pollution, waste, water scarcity, deforestation, and sustainably, will be a cost burden all nations will need to be ready to address. How rapidly Asia embraces sustainability both at the national and business level will significantly impact all plans for a sustainable planet. If Asia embraces sustainability, the planet has a better chance of survival! Today, Asian CEOs from China, India, Japan, Korea, and ASEAN nations strive to achieve economic growth at any cost. This paradigm needs to change towards triple-bottom-line growth and resource stewardship.

A Call to Business Action for the Planet!

The reality of global sustainability challenges with special emphasis on climate-change-related challenges was outlined in the first chapter.

The looming water crisis, global pollution, waste, impacts of deforestation, and rising inequality were highlighted, along with the resultant impact of global warming and climate change.

Twenty-two years after the Rio Earth Summit, the planet's carbon emissions increased from less than twenty-one gigatons in 1992 to around thirty-two gigatons in 2014.[116] Carbon concentrations in the atmosphere increased from less than 250 parts per million to 400 parts per million in March 2015, according to NASA.[117]

The impending catastrophe of global warming, six-metre sea-level rise, and the direct impact on water scarcity and food scarcity are no longer just a possible scenario but the reality humanity will have to face up to, where a two-to-four-degree-Celsius rise in temperature seems inevitable. The inaction of global leaders over the past twenty-two years, despite all the evidence, has led to this crisis.

In chapter 2, the reality in terms of the lack of business response to the emerging crisis was confirmed by the fact that 97 per cent of the world's largest listed corporations do not report on sustainability. The gap between verbal commitments and action amongst most CEOs and businesses, where only around 20 to 30 per cent of those making commitments to embed sustainability

---

[116] Financial Times 13th March 2015 – Source IAEA
[117] NASA – National Aeronautics and Space Administration USA

even remotely did so, is confirmed by many research studies. This status quo of inaction and the resultant impacts on the planet will jeopardise all business and cause great distress to nations and humanity.

In chapter 3, the challenge of internalising strategic corporate sustainability and strategic national sustainability was presented as a concept that would embed sustainability in strategy, as opposed to the current peripheral and bolt-on approach, which has done little to halt or reverse global carbon emissions. The need for creating a cadre of triple-bottom-line mindset leaders was presented as the priority.

In chapter 4, the opportunity to do so by mobilising the 7 Imperatives for Sustainable Business was outlined. The success of enlightened businesses that had followed this path was highlighted, to demonstrate that sustainability-led differentiation and innovation is good for business and the planet. The opportunity to create blue oceans of green market spaces was presented with a step-by-step approach as to how this can be achieved.

In chapter 5, the focus is on a call to urgent action by both business and national leaders. The need for sustainable resource utilisation and installing sustainable business performance indicators (SBPIs) and national sustainability performance indicators (NBPIs) as steps to focus and measure sustainability impact on key challenges was presented.

The planet is at a critical juncture, and the rising influence and financial strength makes it imperative that *business takes the lead* in terms of urgent action for the planet. The time has come for robust public policies and business action. If you are a business leader or aspire to be one, this message is for you.

Today you have a choice to either ignore the message in this book and continue with business as usual, convincing yourself why it's not your responsibility, or make a commitment to pursue sustainable business. If you make that commitment, it's one you're making not only for your business but also for all future generations, including your children and grandchildren.

Today you have the choice - to put this book away and forget its message or make a bold decision to stop the current inaction and embrace strategic corporate sustainability.

BIBLIOGRAPHY

Benn.S, Dunphy. D and Griffiths. A (2007), *enabling change for corporate sustainability: An Integrated Perspective, Australian Journal of Environmental management* - Volume 13 pp.156-157

Blue Ocean Strategy (2005) *https://hbr.org/2004/10/blue-ocean-strategy/ar/1*

Bonn. I and Fisher. J (2011), *Sustainability: The missing ingredient in strategy, Journal of Business strategy,* Vol.32 Iss.1 pp 6

Bonini. S & Görner. S (2014) The Business of Sustainability: Putting it into Practice. McKinsey & Co.

http://www.bloomberg.com/news/2012-09-11/top1000-companies-weild-power-reserved-for-nations.html

Burger. A -'How Government Subsidies Drive Deforestation and Inequality' Triple Pundit 6th April 2015 from a working paper titled 'Subsidies to key commodities driving forest loss-Implications for private climate finance - Will McFarland, Shelagh Whitley and Gabrielle Kissinger March 2015

Cambridge University Institute of Sustainability Leadership Newsletter June 2015

Carlzon. J - Moments of Truth (1987)

Carbon Disclosure Project /Accenture report -Supply Chain Sustainability Revealed: A Country Comparison supply chain reports 2014-15

CERES *the 21st Century Corporation: The Ceres Roadmap for Sustainability (2010) pp. 5*

Chan Kim .W and Mauborgne. R – Blue Ocean strategy – How to Create Uncontested Market Spaces and Make the Competition irrelevant, © 2015 Harvard Business School Publishing Corporation

Chan Kim .W and Mauborgne (2005)– Blue Ocean strategy, Harvard Business school publishing corporation, Page 176-177

Chan Kim & Mauborgne 'As Is' Strategy Canvas – Blue Ocean strategy (2005) pg.23-44

Chan Kim & Mauborgne ERRC Grid – Blue Ocean Strategy (2005) pg.35

Corporate Sustainability – A Progress report 2011, KPMG INTERNATIONAL IN COOPERATION WITH ECONOMIC INTELLIGENCE UNIT

Corporate Sustainability and the United Nations Post-2015 Development Agenda

Crane .K & Mao .Z (2015), Costs of selected policies to address Air Pollution in China © 2015 Rand Corporation

Confino .J (2014) 19 October 2014 -Finance hub from Guardian Sustainable Business

Confino. J, The Guardian 20th January 2015

Drucker .P & Lee .N, Corporate Social Responsibility (2005) John Wiley & sons Inc.

Eccles R.G, Ioannis. I, Serafeim .G (2011), *The Impact of a Corporate Culture of sustainability on Corporate Behaviour and performance*, Harvard Business school working paper (12-035) November 25th, 2011:2-27.

Edie.net 8 July 2015 Matt Field : WWF and Unilever announce campaign to protect one million trees

Epstein's and Roy.M.J (2003), *Making the case for Sustainability, Linking social and environmental performance actions to financial performance*, JCC9 Spring 2003 © Greenleaf publishing:1.

Esty .D (2014), "How to make Wall street notice sustainability leaders", Green Biz.com 2014-09-02

Economist February 17, 2015 – Pollution -The Cost of Clean Air

Ethical Corporation (January 2015) Top Sustainability trends for 2015

Elkington .J (2014) 'Cannibals' with Forks' Best Business books

Elkinton .J & Zeitz. J – The Breakthrough Challenge (2014), Wiley

Forward in Supply Chain Sustainability Revealed: A Country Comparison supply chain reports 2014-15 pp3

Fernando .R (2012),"*Sustainable globalization and Implications for strategic corporate and national sustainability*", Corporate Governance, Vol.12 Iss:4 :586.

FERNANDO. R (2013), '*Singapore -A City in a Garden: A Vision for environmental sustainability*' (01/2013-5382) ©INSEAD Case :12.

Fernando .R (2010), *Sustainable globalization and implications for strategic corporate and national sustainability*, Corporate governance, Vol.12 Iss: 4 :587.

FERNANDO. R (2010), *Sustainable globalization and implications for strategic corporate and national sustainability*, Corporate governance Vol.12 Iss:4:587-594.

FT Wealth summer 2014 – Debate Global inequality pg. 40-41

Financial Times 14 July 2015 'Crude crash holds back shift to renewables'

Financial Times 5th February 2015 Global Debt

Financial Times 13th March 2015 – Source IAEA

Financial Times 19 June 2015 'Pope says multinationals and greed threaten environment'

Financial Times 14 July 2015 'Crude crash holds back shift to renewables'

Financial Times 13th March 2015 - Source IAEA

© Global Strategic Corporate Sustainability Pvt. Ltd 'IDEAS'(2015)

Global Strategic Corporate Sustainability Pvt. Ltd is a sustainability consulting organization set up in 2015.

Global canopy program Forest 500-2015 report (http://www. globalcanopy.org)

Global Water security - Intelligence community assessment ICA 2012-08, 2 February 2012

GE Ecomagination - www.**ge**.com/about-us/**ecomagination**

Globescan and Trucost (2014) - Green biz state of green business

http://www.greenbiz.com/article -Apple, Google and the evolving economics of energy-Greenbiz 13 Feb 2015

Guardian 20th January 2015: How concerned are CEO's about Climate change?

Hepler L. & Grady. B 'Environment as economic threat: How sustainability defines risk, February 4, 2015

Hockerts .K (2001), *What does Corporate Sustainability actually mean from a Business point of view?* paper presented at the Greening of industry Network conference, 21-24th January 2001, Bangkok, Thailand:3.

INSEAD Case 2006 'Strategic corporate social responsibility in the Apparel industry'

INSEAD Case 2008 'MAS Leveraging Corporate Responsibility'

INSEAD Case 2009 'Mabroc Kelani Valley – Creating the Ethical Tea brand of the World'

KPMG/EIU(2011) Corporate Sustainability a progress report

Kotler .P and Chang .N – Corporate social responsibility (2002)

Lancet Medical Journal 23 June 2015, Health and Climate change :Policy responses to protect public health

Laszlo. C. (2003) – The Sustainable Company – *Toward an Integrated Bottom line pg. 15*

Laszlo .C (2003) – The Sustainable Company, *The Stakeholder Mindset and Culture pg45*

Laszlo .C (2008), *Sustainable Value How the World's leading companies are doing well by doing good*, Greenleaf Publishing Ltd. pg15.

Laszlo .C (2011), Embedding Sustainability, The next competitive advantage, Greenleaf Publishing Ltd.

Little. D. A 2005 How leading companies are using sustainability - driven innovation to win Tomorrow's Customers © 2005 Arthur D. Little

Lubin .D .A and Esty .D .C (2010) *The Sustainability Imperative – Lessons from leaders from previous game changing megatrends –* Harvard Business Review May 2010:44-60.

Lux Research - Corporate Sustainability Initiatives lack critical Data and Analytics April 7 2015

Marks and Spencer Plan A - *planareport.marksandspencer.com*

Mckinsey (2011) The Business of sustainability

Mckinsey(2014) global survey results February 2014, Figure 1

Morgan Stanley Corporate Index -*www.msci.com/resources/factsheets/index_fact.../msci-world-index.pdf*

MIT Sloan Management review (MIT SMR) and the Boston Consulting group (BCG) report December 2013 'Sustainability's Next frontier: Walking the Talk on the Sustainability issues that matter most'

NASA – National Aeronautics and Space Administration USA 2015 March

Nidumolu .R, Prahalad .C .K and Rangaswami .M .R (2009), *Why Sustainability is now the key driver of innovation* HBR September 2009: 55-60

Principles of Responsible Investment survey (2014)

Radjou. N and Prabu .J (HBR December 2014) 'What Frugal Innovators Do'

Schiffman .R, Environment 360 July 9th 2015, How can we make people care about climate change?

Singapore – A City in a Garden, A Vision for environmental sustainability (INSEAD Case study 2013) pp. 12

State of Green Business: Business leads in renewable power – Greenbiz 19 March 2015

Standard and Poor Index – *us.spindices.com/indices/equity/sp-500* Strauss. B, Climate Central 9 July 2015 'Coastal Nations, Megacities face 20 Feet of sea rise'

Tesla Motors – *www.teslamotors.com* Toyota Hybrid cars – *www.toyota.com/hybrid-cars*

treehugger – Transportation, Michael Graham Richard 13 July 2015

UCI led study using NASA data 2003-2013 UC Irvine/NASA/JPL-Caltech

UN Global Compact-*https://www.**unglobalcompact**.org*

UN Earth Summit Climate Conference Rio (1992)

UNGC New York July 2012 – source – communication division

UN Global Compact – *A New Era of Sustainability 2010 UN Global Compact – Accenture CEO Study 2010*:12.

UNGC/Accenture (2013) The UN Global Compact-Accenture CEO Study on Sustainability 2013

UN Global compact Accenture CEO survey(2013)'Architects of a Better World'

UN.org -http://www.un.org/news/press/docs/2011/sgsm13372.doc.htm

UN Global Compact Sri Lanka analysis Dec 2012 -Top 100 Global economic entities(2011)

UNGC Corporate blue print https://www.**unglobalcompact**.org

Unilever Sustainable Living Plan – www.**unilever**.com/**sustainable-living**-2014

Unilever CEO Paul Polman message to investors in 2014

Wal-Mart 360 – Co*rporate.**walmart**.com/microsites/globalreport/* ***sustainability360**.html*

World Economic Forum Global competitiveness report 2013

World Economic Forum global agenda councils 'Outlook on the global agenda 2015 pg. 23

World Economic Forum (2015) Global Risks Report; KPMG (2013) Expect the Unexpected.

World Economic Forum global agenda councils 'Outlook on the global agenda 2015 pg. 26-28

World Economic Forum global agenda councils 'Outlook on the global agenda 2015 pg. 14-16, pg. 52-63

World Resources Institute **Water Stress Map** "Source: WRI Aqueduct aqueduct.wri.org"

Yale environment e360 2014 – Global Forest(2014) cover decline by 50% in past 30 years and 52% of Animal species in past 40years

Printed in the United States
By Bookmasters